Cooler By The Lake

A Memoir

Roger Triemstra

FOREWORD BY TOM SKILLING

BANTRY BAY PUBLISHING
CHICAGO + LOS ANGELES

Cooler By The Lake

ISBN 978-1-7352638-6-1

Library of Congress Control Number: 2021924086

All of the events in this memoir are true to the best of the author's memory. Some events have been compressed, and some dialogue has been recreated. It reflects the author's present recollections of experiences over many, many years.

Photos and images are the property of Roger Triemstra, unless otherwise indicated. Cover photo from 123rf.com. WGN promotional images are courtesy of WGN Radio. Walk of Fame photos by Dave Marzullo of WGN Radio. Tom Skilling photo from WGN-TV.

Interior and cover design and layout by Bantry Bay Publishing, Chicago/Los Angeles.

To contact the author or the publisher, email BantryBayPublishing@gmail.com, or call (312) 912-8639.

Table of Contents

Dedications

To my wife, Gerrie, who was a constant support, a true partner, and the love of my life, this book is affectionately dedicated.

To my children, who have traveled with me through my life, I am so proud of each one of you. I hope to leave you with some insight of myself other than as your dad. I dedicate this with much love.

And to my grandchildren and my great-grandchildren, I dedicate this book to all of you who will have faded memories of me, or no memories at all. You are the true extensions of my life and the unforeseen future, and are deeply loved.

And to those of my teachers who believed I was more than a Vulture.

> *Isn't it funny how day by day nothing changes, but when you look back, everything is different.*
>
> – Unknown

Introduction

Over the years, various people told me I should write a book. I didn't, mainly because I didn't think people would be interested enough in my life story.

I still feel that way, but other reasons surfaced that made me reconsider becoming an author. Primarily, my family. Gerrie and I were blessed with four children, 13 grandchildren and 15 great-grandchildren, and I expect the family will continue to grow once I am no longer on this earth.

There wasn't much, if anything, written or known about my grandparents and other ancestors, so I wanted to share my life experiences with my family and they can pass it on to their families and a piece of Gerrie and I will always be memorialized in this book for them.

And for the WGN-TV viewers and WGN Radio listeners, I hope you'll enjoy reading this book and reminiscing about the past.

WGN-TV Meteorologist Tom Skilling

Foreword

I promise you, any and all who have watched, listened to and admired my colleague and veteran WGN meteorologist Rog Triemstra over his iconic 33-year career are going to love this memoir.

Rog was the lead meteorologist at WGN when I arrived on the scene in 1978 and it's interesting now, when there's so much in the news every day about climate change, that Rog was one of the early advocates of climate change awareness. And I am living proof of somebody whose view on the whole subject has changed. Rog and I used to get into debates about climate change. I, as a young forecaster, used to think that when I heard the Arctic was going to melt, boy, you would have to prove that to me, but Rog was way ahead of so many of us.

Having read every word of his memoir multiple times, I can't even imagine the time and research that went into it. It's marvelous — the photos included are wonderful. I've learned things and gained insights into Roger and his family I never knew, even having worked with him over so many years.

Roger's life and that of the Triemstra family are true American success stories. His broadcast career, of which so many in the Chicago area are so wonderfully familiar, is but one facet of a fascinating life, which included years as a highly successful engineer at Amoco Chemical and Kaiser Aluminum and three years as an Air Force meteorologist who briefed pilots at Wright Patterson Air Force Base in Dayton, Ohio, during the Korean War.

I got a kick out of the stories about how Rog became a TV meteorologist. I won't spoil it for you, but it involved a couple of muggings on the streets of Chicago!

But to focus solely on Triemstra's years as a broadcast meteorologist would be to completely understate the range in talents and expertise over his multi-faceted career that extended over more than a half century. Rog is a rare combination of meteorologist and scientist. He holds degrees in engineering from IIT, where he engaged in honors studies, and earned an

MBA from IIT, as well. And, as you'll read, from an early age Rog was also a serial entrepreneur who eventually owned a popular pizza parlor and a recreation center.

Perhaps most important of all, Triemstra is also a devoted father, husband, grandfather and great-grandfather. Before that, he was the devoted (and doted on) fifth child of Lena and Jacob Triemstra and grew up in South Holland, which was settled by Dutch immigrants. Among the fascinating asides in Roger's book is a history of South Holland and the nearby area.

Roger, the dedicated meteorologist he has always been, notes he was born on a day of record heat — 90 degrees on April 11, 1930 — and points out that veteran Chicago weather observer Frank Wachowski found only two other instances of 90-degree heat so early in the season — on April 30, 1942 and April 22, 1980.

The way Rog writes about his late wife Gerrie — the "love of his life" — is so tender and lovely. This was a true love affair that lasted over seven decades of marriage. The affection the two of them enjoyed and the love they shared with their children, grandchildren and great-grandchildren is such an important theme of Roger's book and memoir.

As a fan, it was fun to read Rog's interactions with WGN legends such as Wally Phillips, Bob Collins, Spike O'Dell, Roy Leonard, the inimitable Orion Samuelson, Max Armstrong and, of course, the biggest star of them all, Bozo. The historic tidbit he included about a former WGN-TV sportscaster blew me away.

My biggest takeaway from this book is what a large, rich life Rog has had. Yes, much of it recounts his great successes in broadcasting, but he really pulls back the curtains on his personal life. I'm sure he did this because of his desire for this to be a lasting record of his and Gerrie's lives for future Triemstra generations, but it also gives the rest of us a peek into a life well lived.

Check it out. I think you're going to enjoy it!

Tom Skilling

The Muggings

Getting mugged was the best thing that happened to my career as a radio and TV meteorologist.

It happened twice. Neither time to me, thankfully. There was a morning show on the ABC-TV station (WBKB now WLS) called *Clock-a-Doodle-Day.* It was on 90 minutes each morning and had news and weather for the adults, and entertainment for the kids from "Captain Stubby and the Buccaneers," which was a country-comedy band. The show featured a meteorologist named Warren Culbertson, who did "Weather by Radar," a science segment for children. On his way home after a show in 1962, some thugs beat him up. According to Culbertson:

> *"I was robbed by two men one evening while I was in Chicago. I had just pulled up to my apartment, got out of the car and was met by these men. I got a couple of teeth knocked out, but fortunately, they picked the wrong pocket and didn't get much from me."*

I had appeared as a guest weathercaster on a few occasions, and I need to back up a little and explain how that happened.

It was Armed Forces Day at Lockbourne Air Force Base, and an open house was held. In attendance was a TV weatherman from Columbus, Ohio, and we struck up a conversation about weather and my potential future after the Air Force. He was a former teacher of Clint Youle, the Chicago NBC (WNBQ, Channel 5) weatherman, who was the first weatherman to do forecasts on a national TV show. Clint also served in the Air Force and was trained in meteorology. I had heard that Clint had received a 10-year, $100,000 per year contract and this was appealing to me, since I was not aware that the weather industry could be a profitable career path. That was huge money back then. I'd always thought that anyone serious about meteorology would not go into television; they'd use their degree for research, or as a forecaster for a private firm or for the airlines. But the thought that stations would pay that kind of money for something I was well-qualified to do made me look in that direction. It didn't hurt that I was a ham and had a gift of gab that had served me well up to that point in my life.

The visiting weatherman from Columbus suggested that I stop in to see Clint on my next trip to Chicago to see if there were any work opportunities at Channel 5. Nothing came from that meeting, so I reached out to Channel 2 and Channel 7. The weatherman at Channel 2, P.J. Hoff, who was in his 60s, served an older, more mature audience and they were not interested in bringing in a younger fill-in for him. However, Channel 7 did give me an audition, but I received no employment offer...just yet.

Upon my return from the service, there was a need for a backup weather person for Warren Culbertson at ABC's Channel 7. It was the only Chicago station utilizing radar with its forecasts at that time and since I was skilled in forecasting with radar and had already completed an audition, I was hired as Warren's backup. When he was mugged, I filled in for about six weeks on the regular news show. I also ended up doing several fill-ins with Alex Dreier, who was known as Chicago's "Man on the Go." He was the city's top TV anchor during his years on Channel 5.

After Warren recovered and came back to work, I continued to fill in at ABC for a few years. Some folks at WGN knew of me and I filled in on Channel 9 from time to time for lead weatherman Harry Volkman. In 1965, he was mugged. Harry got beat up when he stopped at a Dunkin' Donuts on his way home. I took over for Harry while his facial bruises and scars healed. My filling in for mugged weathermen became a joke and was written up in one of the gossip columns: "Don't get Triemstra as your backup because he'll pitch onions at you."

WGN was pleased with my performance and asked me to be the regular back up for Harry and do weather on the weekends. That began my long tenure at WGN, but it was only part time.

When I started filling in at WGN-TV, it was on weekends only. I finished at Kaiser on Friday afternoons and I'd get to the studio on West Bradley Place by 8:30 p.m. to start setting up the big weather map. I'd have to use a ladder to reach some of the areas to write in the temperatures, the "L" and "H" for low- and high-pressure areas, draw the fronts and other graphics. I did the 10 p.m. weather. Later, they asked if I would do the five o'clock show, too, so I worked it out with Kaiser to get off a little early.

I also started doing weather for a Lansing radio station, WLNR, which was a low-power FM station. WLNR stood for "West Lansing Near Railroad." One of the owners of the station was my cousin, Joe Van Schouwen. Before I went to Kaiser in the morning, I would drive over to Lansing and give the weather forecast. They thought I was a big deal because I was on Channel 9. I got a few bucks, but I did it more as a favor to my cousin. Joe was a champion drummer in high school and, believe it or not, we had a Dixieland band called "Joe Banana and his Bunch — Music with a Peel." I played trombone, and later, I actually took the trombone and played it on the air when I worked at WGN.

Playing at my son's wedding.

A Day in the Life

Keeping with my mantra of "Find an opportunity and take it," there was a period in the late '70s when I took a lot of opportunities. Here's what my typical day looked like during that time.

- *6:45 a.m. Arrive at WLNR Lansing radio studio for a 7:00 a.m. weather show.*
- *7:30 a.m. Home for breakfast.*
- *8 a.m. WGN Wally Phillips show call-in.*
- *8:30 a.m. Drove to Kaiser in Dolton for my engineering job and did some radio shows from there.*
- *Occasionally drove home for lunch.*
- *Back to Kaiser after lunch and more radio if needed for WGN.*
- *3 p.m. Back home to change for WGN-TV and drive to Bradley Place for the 5:00 p.m. show.*
- *Sometimes drove home to tuck the kids into bed.*
- *8:30 p.m. Drove back to WGN-TV for the 10 p.m. show – sometimes later if a Cubs game was on the air.*
- *Occasionally taught economics at IIT in Chicago.*
- *During these years, I also co-owned Pipes and Pizza and Lynwood Sports Center, was a village trustee, served as president of the South Holland Industrial Commission and taught Bible classes.*

The schedule took a toll. While driving home at night after WGN-TV, I hit a retaining wall and knocked the mirror off my car. Other times, I missed the exit for South Holland. It became too dangerous to drive myself home, so my sister Emily drove with me, and once my kids could drive, they also helped. Occasionally, friends I brought to see the studio would get me home safely.

Even with everything else I had going on, I found time to run for South Holland Village Trustee in 1973. I won the election and actually drew more votes than the mayor did. Politics wasn't for me, though. I was asked to serve another term, but I declined. I found it very difficult to implement any changes. It was too political.

Through all of this, I was very protective of my commitment to my kids as a father, as the leader of the family. I don't think I ever made a decision on anything without first considering, "What does this do to my family? What does it do to my wife?" My kids knew I was busy all the time. But they also knew that it was being done for the good of our family.

In 1982, I left Kaiser and after working part time for 17 years at WGN-TV and Radio, I went full time. I stayed another 16 years, retiring in 1998 after a total of 33 years there. I'd like to think the reasons for my longevity and success at WGN included my authenticity. It was something management stressed for all on-air talent, and I was as authentic as they came. I also tried to relate how the weather affected the average person going through their day. There'd be reams of complicated information coming from the National Weather Service that I had to digest in creating forecasts, but I tried to boil it down to whether people should take their raincoat with them to work.

Weather forecasting is a thankless job. People always remembered when I'd miss a forecast, but they always forgot when I was right. My accuracy was pretty good — I'd say I was right 90 to 95 percent of the time on the 24-hour forecasts. That five to 10 percent I'll blame mostly on Lake Michigan. An article in the *Milwaukee Journal-Sentinel* spelled it out well:

> *"It is not easy to forecast the weather on Lake Michigan. For one thing, it is huge: more than 22,000 square miles; 308 miles long and 118 miles wide with an average water depth of 280 feet. There are few sensors feeding data to the National Weather service computers, which record wave height, direction and frequency, air and water temperature, wind speed and direction, dew point and humidity levels. Weather buoys are dropped into the lake by the U.S. Coast Guard each spring and removed in late fall. Meteorologists rely heavily on ship captains so there are many variables making it a challenge to forecast weather happening across Lake Michigan. Satellites are used to learn ice locations, winds, and lake water temperatures. Many of the estimated 6,000 shipwrecks at the bottom of Lake Michigan were weather victims."*

Lake Michigan can produce tremendous shifts and changes in the weather with little warning, and that goes for both sides of the lake. And occasionally, I just didn't want to believe the data. Maybe it had been a stretch of bad weather and you're looking for a ray of hope and your own feelings and opinions get in the way of accuracy.

Which brings me to the *Old Farmer's Almanac.* You have no idea how much grief the Almanac caused for me and any professional meteorologist, because it's all witchcraft. How can you put out a magazine and give a whole year's forecast while the professionals aren't sure what's happening next month? And yet, a lot of people buy it. And the groundhog telling us when winter is ending? If you want to have a muskrat determine what the weather's going to be, have at it.

There's a lot of science and technology in meteorology and there are also a lot of old wives' tales. There was a guy in Milwaukee forecasting the weather by how deep the perch were swimming. How ridiculous is that? The depth of a perch is going to tell you what kind of weather you're going to get? What it tells you is that the perch are down there because that's where the food is.

Some old wives tales are valid, though, such as when someone, usually an older person, tells you they can feel it in their bones that a storm is coming. There's science behind that. If there's arthritis or a broken bone doesn't heal right, air pockets can form, and some people really feel the change in air pressure that accompanies a change in the weather.

What bothers me, though, is when the broadcast weather people — I won't call them meteorologists because not all of them are — clown around with the forecasting. I did my share of clowning around, but never at the expense of the forecast because, at its extremes, meteorology really is about life and death. It was important that I present all the information in an entertaining way, and as big of a ham as I was, I had no problem there. But I believed it wasn't as important to entertain as it was to inform, and I think people who followed my forecasts saw me as believable. I wasn't the movie-star anchorman type. I was just a guy who was losing his hair.

About that departing hair, management wanted me to get a

hairpiece. I refused. They even had a guy come in after the 10 o'clock news, a wig stylist, to try different wigs on me. This would be 10:30, 11:00 p.m., and I wasn't in the mood for it. I told him, "I'm not going to get a wig. Just understand that." He said, "But they want you to, and they're paying for it." It was around 700 bucks. I told management, "You know what? I am not going to wear a raccoon on my head, whether you like it or not. If I get fired, I get fired. I am not going to wear a wig, sorry." That was the end of that. And you know what, being bald is now a normal thing on television. There are more bald guys than ever on the air.

Going bald was never a problem for me. I think it started during the service and I was told hair loss happened because of the service hats we had to wear. These were the ones with a visor, similar to police hats. And those hats usually had a plastic lining. You're generating heat and your hair follicles do not get enough air, and the theory was that tended to increase hair loss. And I think there's a lot of truth in that because before that, I had wavy, blonde hair. In high school, I was called "The Blonde Tiger." Girls wanted to run their fingers through it.

Hair or no hair, I didn't care. I always had a strong personality and it didn't matter. If you can't evaluate what's inside my head and what makes me tick, what is important in my life, then I don't want anything to do with it, period. No toupee for me.

Makeup was another story. I was such an old school guy, wearing makeup is what my four sisters did. The "I'm no sissy, I'm a Vulture" mentality from my youth was still there. But the lights in the studio were so bright that if I didn't apply some pancake up on my balding head, it would shine like a light bulb. So, I did it; I used the makeup, but I was bad at applying it and they brought in a professional. Before I left the studio to go home, I'd go into the men's room and wash my face clean.

The next person who puts makeup on me will be the mortician. My casket will only be open a few minutes for my kids to see me, and then we're going to close it and the same quilt Gerrie had made and was draped over her casket will be over mine on one end. On the other end will be the American flag for my service as a military man.

Leaving TV behind to do radio full-time was an easy decision. Radio provides much more freedom. For television, I'd drive 30 miles to get to the studio, spend 30 minutes preparing, and then was on the air for three minutes in a very tight and structured format. For radio, I could — and did — do my forecasts from anywhere in the world by telephone, and I enjoyed the opportunities to banter with my colleagues, a few of whom I'll mention below.

Wally Phillips

Wally was the biggest radio star in Chicago, number one in the morning slot. He had the highest ratings of anybody for two decades, and for whatever reason, he took a liking to me and vice versa. We had some things in common: He had been in the Air Force. He was about five years older and was in high school during World War II and dropped out to join. I was in the Air Force in Ohio when he was working for WLW in Cincinnati and I always listened to him there. We reminisced about Ohio.

We each had been married to one woman, although he married the same woman three times. But our personalities couldn't have been more different. On the air, you would have thought Wally was the most outgoing, fun, life-of-the-party guy, but after his shift, he'd sit alone in the cafeteria. A lot of his co-workers took that to mean he was aloof, but after doing four straight, intense hours of radio, he probably just needed a breather. Well, I'd just go sit down and talk to him. He appreciated that.

Wally liked my sense of humor and no matter where I was in the world, he wanted me to do the weather on his show. Whether I was in Antarctica or the Amazon or Hawaii or wherever, he wanted me to call in. I was happy to do it, even on vacation. I would always take care of Wally.

I don't remember if this started with Wally, but it sounds like something he'd think of. When I was out and about and calling in to his show with the weather, often from a phone booth, somebody came up with the idea of turning it into a "Find Roger" contest. I'd give hints about my location and the first person who found me while I was on the air would get a prize.

Bob Collins

After Wally stopped doing mornings and moved to afternoons in 1986, he was replaced by Bob Collins. They couldn't have been more different in their types of talent and personalities. Bob's folksy style and cackle laugh led him to be known as "Uncle Bobby" to his fans, and he continued Wally's number one ranking.

Bob was also different in how he included me in his show. He only wanted me to do the weather and didn't integrate me into the show as much as Wally had. That was okay with me. I wasn't there to be a funny guy. I was there to do the weather. Bob and I developed a love-hate relationship, but it wasn't a serious one. It played well on the air. One day, though, Bob took it too far. He started making fun of my weather forecasts. He may have thought he was being funny, but what I heard was him denigrating my technical competence as a meteorologist. There were other broadcast meteorologists, or just weathermen, who tried to make the weather funny. I never did. I screwed around a lot on the air, but not with the forecast. People trusted me as a weatherman who knew what he was talking about, but who could also be screwy at times.

When Collins went over the line, I said to myself, "Who does this guy think he is? He's just a disc jockey." I wasn't going to be disrespected like that and I walked off the show; just got up and went home.

It wasn't long — it may have been the same day — he called and apologized and asked me to come back. He said, "I made a mistake. You've contributed way more to the show than I ever gave you credit for." For Bob, who was not humble, that was a big thing to do.

From then on, Bob and I did a lot of bantering and we developed a fun relationship on the air. He called me "Old Blue Eyes." Bob would give it to me, I would give it to him right back, and he was OK with that.

As different as we were, we liked each other. He would come to my cottage in Michigan and we did things together. We had a common interest in aviation. He loved to fly and one of the things he admired about me and liked hearing about was my service with the Strategic Air Command.

The afternoon he died in the plane crash, February 8, 2000, I was at home. I'd been retired for nearly two years and received a call from Spike O'Dell to come to the station. Spike was the afternoon guy and a lot of us who had known and worked with Bob gathered in the studio to mourn together and on the air. It was a very emotional time, and a great loss for Chicago.

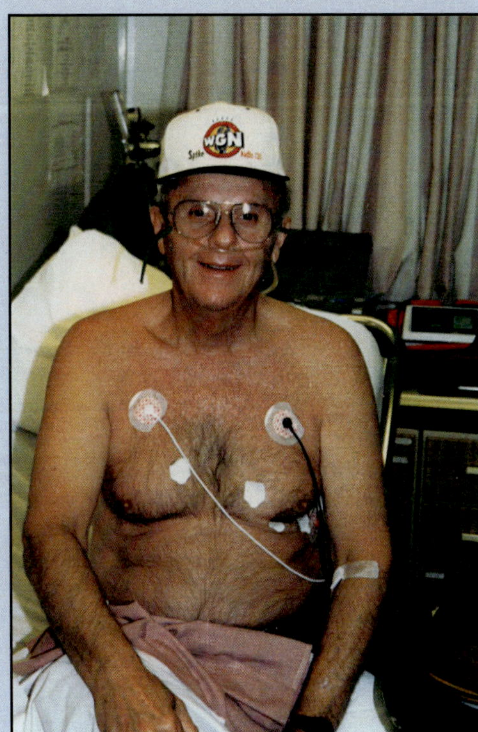

When we were back in the States after my heart episode on a WGN listener cruise, Bob Collins wanted to see a photo of me in the hospital, all wired up after the stent procedure.

Spike O'Dell

Spike moved to mornings to take over after Bob's death. That had to be a hard thing to handle, but he did it well, and continued the high ratings that the morning show was known for. Spike was a funny guy, had a great sense of humor, a great laugh, and I could make him laugh. He'd give it back to me, too, and I put up with a lot of stuff, but I genuinely liked him and liked working with him.

A quote about Spike on the WGN website stated:

> *"The key to Spike's success has been his dedication to the show, WGN, and his listening audience. Spike is known for being personable to everyone he comes in contact with both on and off the air. He's very genuine and in the day and age of automation he brought a real human element to all of us. Spike found it ironic that he made a living doing what he went to detention for in high school ... talking."*

I can't say that I enjoyed working with everyone, especially some of the TV anchormen, but I could always fake it. There was no faking needed with Spike.

Spike had a nickname for me: "You old goat." We had a great team on Spike's show, including Spike's producer, Tracy Heuvelman, and traffic reporter, Anne Maxfield. We shared some great times and outings together, and remain friends to this day.

Spike had a funny way of always getting the last word — he would hang up on me as I was in mid-sentence. I'll let Spike get the last word again, as he wanted to share a few memories of our WGN years.

> *How the heck can I write just a couple of paragraphs about Roger Triemstra?!?*
>
> *First of all, I love the old goat. I know he loves me, too. A lot of*

people wouldn't think that the way we went after each other on the air. I assure anyone reading this, it was all good-natured and in fun. We loved to get after one another. It wasn't always on the air, either. Some of the best pranks we pulled on each other were off the air. We loved to argue about sports, and politics, and our favorite conversations concerned religion. Roger is one of those people who not only professes his beliefs, but practices them, too. Kind of rare anymore. I went to a Christian college with a minor in Bible and married a preacher's daughter, and Roger was very active in his church life, so we could get pretty deep into theology and challenge each other on the fine points. Of course, we both had to argue who was right but again, it was done in fun and respect.

Now, sports was a different animal. We were on opposite ends of the spectrum with Roger being a huge White Sox fan, and I was a dyed-in-the-wool Cubs fan! You just prayed with every new season your team would finish ahead of the other's, because we had a standing bet that whoever's team finished ahead, would be treated to a nice steak dinner by the other. The needling was relentless.

When I did the afternoon show, the crew we had became pretty tight. We just clicked. Tracy was my producer, Annie and Linc in the traffic department, Steve Bertrand and Tom Petersen in the newsroom. And of course, the man who saved America during the war with his weather forecasts and fought with his typewriter, Roger! We all became great friends and hung out with each other, and actually enjoyed each other's company. We decided to go watch a Cubs game together at Wrigley Field one afternoon, and Roger kept complaining how hard it was going to be to sit in THAT field with CUBS FANS! So... I decided to have some fun with him. I called up Frank in the Wrigley Field ticket office and told him that I wanted the absolute WORST seat in the house on the left side. He complied. So, we all went together to the game, but when we got there, Roger noticed that his seat was different than ours. We were

all sitting right over the Cub's dugout, and Roger had the VERY last seat, as far as you could go in the last row of the upper deck! Ha! Hilarious! I actually have a picture of all of us waving at Roger WAY UP there from our great seats. Of course, I went up and got him and brought him down to sit with the rest of us.

There are SO many stories I could tell about our time together. The phone calls with him when I would hang up on him and just leave a dial tone. (He never caught on to that. Ha!) The time he was talking to me on the air while driving to his cottage in Michigan and was pulled over by a State Trooper. I told him to let me talk to the trooper. Roger thought I was going to try and talk the trooper out of a ticket because he was giving the weather forecast to the entire Midwest on the radio, but NO! I told the trooper to write him up just for being ugly and being a Sox fan. I also told him to go kick a taillight out and give him another ticket for that. And so on, and so on. After a while, the trooper caught on to what was happening and actually had fun with it, too. It was unbelievably funny, and all on the air! You can't plan for stuff like that to happen. Priceless! To top it off, the trooper did end up giving him a ticket for speeding, which made it all even funnier. Roger just couldn't believe that he actually got a ticket! He had it out for that cop. So, on the one-year anniversary of Roger getting that ticket, we arranged to have that very trooper deliver Roger donuts at his cottage, another hilarious moment. They both buried the hatchet then and there. The trooper was a good sport about it all.

Roger loved to tell everyone that he was the best weather forecaster in Chicago and everyone else in the biz were only rookies. We let him believe that. In truth, maybe he was.

Looking back on it all, Roger was simply a hoot to work with. I was SO lucky to be able to work at such an incredible radio station with an overflow of talent. We were the best in the biz and the ratings backed it up. He was a big part of the success of my show.

Roger was and remains a good friend, a confidant, a tremendous figure in Chicago and his hometown community. He's an awesome family man and was a faithful husband to Gerrie (the sweetest person you would ever meet) for over 70 years! Roger was never at loss for a wise crack, and he is a Godly man.

The only criticism I could offer about him is that he's a White Sox fan. GO Cubs!

Love you, Roger.

Spike O'Dell

Spike and I aboard the "Yacht Lyle Dean."

Jack Brickhouse

One of the few guys I was in awe of was Jack. He did play-by-play for the Cubs and White Sox for decades, and I think he knew I was a huge White Sox fan. Now and then an athlete would show up at the station and be on the air with Jack during one of his reports. Jack always made sure he introduced me to him, and that was a thrill for me especially if it was a hockey player. I was more of a hockey nut than anything else.

Another sports guy of note at WGN was Wendell Smith, known for his colorful sport jackets, which I teased him about. Wendell was one of the first, if not the first, African-American sportswriter for a major daily newspaper, *The Chicago American,* and in the mid-'60s, he joined WGN. But Wendell's real claim to fame was that he introduced Brooklyn Dodgers General Manager Branch Rickey to Jackie Robinson.

Tom Skilling

Tom is the epitome of a radio and television meteorologist. He's very well-qualified. I was the chief meteorologist at Channel 9 and we needed a backup. Tom auditioned and was hired. I had nothing to do with him coming to WGN. The only thing I did was accept him wholly and with open arms. I think he somewhat looked at me as a father figure. To this day, Tom is one of the most proficient and technologically competent meteorologists on the air.

When WGN-TV and radio split, I mostly stayed with radio and Tom became the chief meteorologist for TV. I always felt more comfortable on radio and felt it was a better showcase for my talent and personality. Tom, along with being one of the best there is, is a great guy. He has never been anything but ultra-kind to me and ultra-respectful of me.

We had many conversations about weather, climate change and global warming and I enjoyed these chats immensely. Tom has been in the forefront of discussions about climate change-fueled extreme weather and participated in a conference in Washington, D.C., urging Congress to act to curb global warming. He spoke about this conference on Bob Sirott's WGN Radio show. Bob commented *"What gets me, Tom, is there are still people who don't think it's real, and I don't get it. You see the floods, the fires, the extreme heat on the news. I think the problem with this country these days, on not just the climate change issue but on many controversial issues, is it's impossible to change the position of some people, no matter what facts you give them. Don't you find that to be true and very frustrating?" Tom replied, "Oh yeah, and you know something, Bob, I am living proof of somebody whose view on the whole subject has changed. I remember Rog Triemstra and I used to get into debates about climate change. Rog was very much talking about it decades ago and I, as a young forecaster, used to think when I heard the Arctic was going to melt, boy, you would have to prove that to me. Well, it's happening!"*

I told you so.

There are so many others I worked with, too many to list, some of whom were both professional and personal friends, such as Wayne Vriesman. Wayne was general manager of WGN for many years, and I'd often sit in his office and chat. It was one of those executive offices with glass walls and people would think I was getting called on the carpet for something I'd done or said on the air. But Wayne and I talked about personal things, like what time we were getting together for dinner, or when he and his family were coming over to our cottage. Wayne was a pleasure to work for and with, and I appreciated him.

Wayne was especially helpful on one of the trips where Gerrie and I were escorting WGN listeners, we flew from the U.S. to London, then boarded a cruise ship with ports of call in France, Spain, Portugal and Gibraltar. On an excursion to Paris, I started feeling chest pains, but I didn't think it was anything to worry about and we continued our trip. Back at sea, the pains got worse, and I had to say something. The ship

When I had a second TIA (transient ischemic attack) in 1999, Spike sent me a homemade get-well card. He couldn't resist a dig at my preference for the White Sox over the Cubs. This was a year after I retired, and it meant a lot to me that Spike still considered me part of the "family."

physician called for a helicopter, and they airlifted Gerrie and me to a Portuguese hospital for tests. This wasn't like modern hospitals where there's a helipad on the roof and a bunch of people rush out with a gurney and take you down to the ER. The helicopter landed some distance from the hospital and a car took me to the hospital, which looked like something out of the 1930s. The driver pulled up in front.

I said, "What do I do now?"

He said, "You go in." There was no wheelchair or anyone to greet us. We walked up some steps where there was a closed door. It had a big brass knocker, so I struck it a few times, and someone came to the door.

"Who are you?" they asked.

"I'm the guy from the boat."

"Oh, OK, come on in, I'll take you to your room."

More stairs, and a doctor is now walking beside me, listening to my chest with a stethoscope. I don't know if I'm dying or what's going on, but he has me walking up and down these stairs and tells me, "You keep repeating 'I can walk and talk.'" So, I do, and he keeps listening, and that was my stress test! It reminded me of the *Carol Burnett Show,* where Tim Conway played a doctor. There was a certain amount of humor in it, but then the doctor tells me they'll get me prepped for surgery.

"Oh, no," I told him, "there won't be any knives coming around me." I'd already started planning to fly back to Chicago. They tried to talk me out of it, telling me I could die in flight, but I was more concerned about dying in that hospital. Wayne Vriesman made the arrangements and we flew to Chicago. When we landed at O'Hare, they took me directly to a hospital and they put stents in my arteries and that was that. I was fine.

My next medical adventure didn't happen on the deck of a ship, it happened under a deck at our home in Highland, Indiana. I'd crawled under it to do some work when I started feeling chest pains.

In addition, I couldn't move my left side. I dragged myself out from under the deck and crawled up some steps to a sliding glass door. I tapped on it for Gerrie to help me. She thought I was joking and waved me off. I kept trying to get her attention and she finally knew something was wrong. I'd had another TIA. Once again, I recovered quickly.

A TWISTER-TRACKING ADVENTURE

Unlike the hit movie "Twister," there were no airborne trucks, there were no flying cows, and if they had spotted a tornado, they would have viewed it from miles away, rather than from the same distance you'd view a Picasso.

CLTV chief meteorologist **Tim McGill**, CLTV photojournalist **Brad Piper** and WGN Radio senior staff meteorologist **Roger Triemstra** chased tornadoes for a week in May. But they did not find themselves scurrying for cover. In fact, despite driving 2,500 miles through Missouri, Iowa, Oklahoma and Kansas, they didn't even see a tornado.

Nonetheless, the tornado chase gave the threesome the opportunity to study weather firsthand. "The more you learn about storms, the better able you are to predict them," says Triemstra, who called in reports about his trip to WGN.

For McGill, the outing provided clips for "Tracking the Twister," a half-hour special that aired on CLTV May 22, 25 and 26.

It was McGill's third tornado special since joining CLTV four years ago. His 1993 show about tornado safety, "Season of Fear," won an Emmy.

"Tracking the Twister" featured dramatic video clips from the National Weather Service and other tornado chasers. And the program profiled Wakita, Okla., the town where part of "Twister" was filmed.

"With the movie 'Twister' coming out, we thought there would be a lot of interest in this subject matter," says McGill, who had never gone on a group chase before. "We knew there was no guarantee we'd see a funnel cloud. The odds are really against you."

Most of the thunderstorms happened at night. "You can't really chase at night because it's too dangerous," McGill says. "Also, the visuals aren't as good unless the sky is illuminated with lightning, and that is rare. What you want is a storm over the plains in the middle of the afternoon."

Since joining CLTV, McGill has been trying to accompany College of DuPage meteorology professor Paul Sirvatka on one of his regular tornado-chasing trips. Scheduling conflicts stood in the way in the past, but McGill finally was able to join the group of 14 chasers, mostly college students.

Triemstra's studies of the weather have taken him from Antarctica to Alaska to the Amazon. He's seen a lot. But there's one thing he's never laid eyes on.

"I've been doing weather reports since 1954, and in all these years, I've never seen a tornado," he says. "But I plan to stay in contact with Paul Sirvatka. If he plans another trip, maybe I'll go, if there's a good chance to see one."

CLTV's "Tracking the Twister" showed up-close footage of tornadoes (large photo). In preparation for the TV special, CLTV and WGN Radio meteorologists went on a tornado chase, during which WGN's Roger Triemstra encountered a microburst that uprooted a tree in El Dorado, Kan.

In June of 1996, I joined fellow meteorologists Tim McGill of CLTV and Paul Sirvatka of the College of DuPage on a tornado chasing trip across four states.

While I was still working full-time as an engineer at Kaiser and part-time on WGN-TV, I also did the morning weather on our South Side station, which announced the fact via newspaper ads.

This newspaper ad shows there was more than one "Mr. T" on television in the 1980s. It's interesting to compare the hand-drawn graphics we used in the '80s with the sophisticated computer graphics in use today.

ABOVE: *One of the many newspaper ads promoting the WGN-TV news team.*
BELOW: *Jack Brickhouse and I were celebrity bartenders at the "World's Largest Office Party," a fund-raising event to benefit the Neediest Children's Fund.*

At another "World's Largest Office Party," Santa tried to share his beard with my bald head, hoping it would take root. It did not.

ABOVE: *"Clearing the wires" — gathering weather reports from the teletypes to prepare my forecast for WGN-TV.* BELOW: *The WGN-TV news set in 1977. Marty McNeeley is in the center and sports anchor Bill Frink is at right.*

Bozo the Clown

My kids never looked at me as a celebrity. I was just their dad who happened to be on TV and radio. The biggest celebrity in Chicago, by far, was Bozo the Clown. The wait for tickets to the *Bozo's Circus* show was something like eight to 10 years. The joke, which probably was true, was if a parent wanted their child to be on the Bozo show, they had to put their name in at birth.

The Triemstra kids had an "in" and were often in the audience for the show but, because they were "WGN kids," they were never chosen for the Buckets game. A boy and girl were selected from the studio audience by the Magic Arrows to toss a ping-pong ball into a series of numbered buckets, each farther away, until they missed. If they made the winning toss into the sixth bucket, they won a prize, usually a bike or some cash or something pretty nice. But the Magic Arrows never pointed at my kids.

They had a lot of fun, though, in the studios when the show wasn't on, playing around backstage with the Bozo drums and the buckets and Garfield Goose. What they quickly realized was how much better things look on TV than in person. The sets for the Bozo show and the newscasts were not as substantial as they appeared on television. The props Frazier Thomas used, the colorful puppets that looked like they were made of gold? They were cardboard or paper and were barely holding together.

Ray Rayner used a real duck for his morning cartoon show, *Ray Rayner and his Friends*. Chelveston the Duck would wander around the set as the cameras followed him and music played. The duck would often be delivered to the studio the night before the show, and some of our crew members would let him out of his cage and then scramble to catch him before the news started. A lot of foolishness happened off camera and behind the scenes.

I would often be asked to make appearances to speak about the weather and my career, and I rarely said no.

Serving as a charity auctioneer.

When the King and Queen of Holland visited Chicago, Gerrie and I, being residents of South Holland and of Dutch descent, were asked to attend a reception at Navy Pier welcoming the royal couple.

Being a media personality presented many opportunities, such as throwing out the first pitch at a Gary Railcats game, racing on a Hobiecat on Lake Michigan, and speeding in a NASCAR race car at Richard Petty's Driving Experience in Brooklyn, Michigan.

The Chicago White Sox provided me with a great deal of joy over the years, no more so than 2005, the year of my 75th birthday, when the Sox won the World Series.

AT LEFT: *I celebrated with Southpaw, the Sox mascot.*

CENTER LEFT: *Gerrie and I with the World Series trophy*

BELOW: *Three generations of Triemstra Sox fans with Cheri and family*

Celebrating the World Series Champions with two Sox legends: Bill "Moose" Skowron on my right and Billy Pierce on my left.

A 1985 photo of my home weather studio featured in the Calumet Daily News.

Every Fourth of July, the Tree-Mendus Fruit Farm in Eau Claire, Michigan, hosted the International Cherry Pit Spitting Contest. It was created in 1974 by Tree-Mendus owner, Herb Teichman, shown above with me, as a way to draw attention to the Southwest Michigan cherry industry and his U-Pick farm. Top right: I am winding up to spit a pit, and did pretty well, maybe 40 or 50 feet, although the world record set in 2004 was over 93 feet. Above: Herb with Uncle Bobby, who helped put the contest on the map and provided the "spit-by-spit" commentary.

PumpkinFest was an annual fundraising and food drive benefit hosted by WGN Radio at the Goebbert Pumpkin Patch near Hampshire, Illinois.
BELOW, MIDDLE: *Either Bob Collins and I were underdressed, or Roy Leonard was overdressed.*

RIGHT: *Some of my grandchildren joined me at PumpkinFest.*

Gerrie and I are joined by Orion "Big O" Samuelson at right, and one of the artists who drew my weather maps for me at WGN-TV.

WGN-TV anchorman Jack Taylor and I attended a Duck and Pheasant Dinner in 1975.

Illinois Governor James "Big Jim" Thompson poses with me at a Navy Pier gala.

The Spike O'Dell Show crew in 1995. Standing behind Spike left to right: Me, Anne Maxfield, Steve Bertrand, Tracy Heuvelman, Randy Minkoff and Milt Owens.

If the weatherman brings an umbrella to the ballgame, so should you. This was August 8, 1988, the first night game at Wrigley Field. It was called after three and-a-half innings.

Weather

WGN meteorologists wired to the National Weather Service keep Chicagoland aware and ready

When arctic cold rolls down from Canada or thunderstorms blow up from the Gulf of Mexico, Chicagoans turn to WGN's Weather Team to make sense of the swift changes.

Roger Triemstra

Diane Clarke

When disastrous weather strikes Chicagoland, listeners know WGN will be the first to broadcast the complete picture. Roger and Diane are networked 24 hours a day with the National Weather Service in the studio and at home.

WGN Radio is one of the few stations in the nation to have an exclusive on-staff team. Our forecast professionals carry degrees in Meteorology, are backed by the latest forecasting technology and have a complete understanding of Chicago's unique weather patterns. This allows them to give not only the most accurate forecast available, but also information on how the day's weather picture may affect listener plans.

Extensive knowledge and service make WGN the only choice for listeners in doubt about the look of the day. Brighten your business' day by sponsoring WGN Weather.

Wally Phillips

Tap into the credibility of a Chicagoland legend

The Big Story, The Big Star, The Big Laugh . . . they're all part of the continuing history of the Wally Phillips legend. If you grew up in the Chicagoland area, chances are you grew up with Wally . . . helping people, making you laugh, telling you everything you needed to know.

Information, Travel, and the "Neediest Kids Christmas Fund" are just a few of the hallmarks of Wally's current shows. What? Where? How? When? Wally finds out. Everything everyone needs, and wants, to know. A cozy bed and breakfast in Wisconsin? A family trip to Disney World? Skiing in Europe? Wally's experts can help with the itinerary. And underlying it all: the caring, helping, human qualities that raise over a million dollars each year – contributions from Boy Scout Troops, everyday people and major corporations – for the Kids fund.

So, remember, if you're packing for Borneo, looking for an obscure birthday gift, or selling your product, Wally Phillips always delivers.

WGN AM RADIO 720

Bob Collins

Giving Chicagoland a jump start on the day

Over the years, Bob Collins has become known to Chicagoland as "Uncle Bobby," everyone's best friend. His listeners feel as comfortable talking to "Uncle Bobby" as they would their next-door neighbor.

Bob is quick to take up the concerns of his listeners, and is not afraid to address the hot issues with high level politicians and leaders in business. The skilled morning crew provides all the news, weather, sports and traffic information needed to start the day. They make sure listeners not only get the "what" but the "why" as well.

By the end of the week Bob and the morning crew have created the right blend of information and entertainment to get listeners ready for the weekend.

Bob Collins is Chicago's #1 radio man. His listeners make a point of spending their mornings with him and their money on the products he advertises.

Spike O'Dell

They Like Spike

Bright, young, with two kids, two cars, a golf bag and the 'burbs, he's a fan of the Beatles, and of Ol' Blue Eyes, too. He's the all American guy, the boy next door, and not afraid to say so.

He calls his show "The Spike O'Dell Radio Experiment"– the "50,000 watt Love Pump"– and that's not a bad description of Spike's unpredictability, spontaneity and infectious warmth and humor that he communicates to all his listeners.

Whether it's traffic, weather, news or sports information, he's on top of the story. Spike is always looking for a way to get listeners home with a smile. There's a "down home" and caring feeling to everything Spike does, and that includes his attitude toward every listener he talks to, every prize he gives away, and every commercial he reads.

Orion & Max
Samuelson Armstrong

Orion Samuelson and Max Armstrong bring listeners comprehensive news on current financial trends. From up-to-the-minute market reports and coverage of trading action to agricultural developments at local, state, national and global levels, Orion and Max deliver all the business information Chicagoland wants and needs.

Orion was a Public Director of the Chicago Board of Trade, and is the only broadcaster to receive two Oscars in agriculture. He travels extensively to cover the issues first-hand. Max has served as a Public Director on the board of the Mid-American Commodity Exchange in Chicago and was the first broadcaster invited to travel overseas with the then-Secretary of Agriculture, John Block. A combined fifty years of solid reporting experience has earned Orion and Max sharp insight on the economy.

When you buy our team you are buying a precious commodity – their credibility. Put your message in the hands of Chicagoland's trusted business experts.

NCP 91⅛ UK 17⅝ GTE 21⅛

WGN AM RADIO 720

Robert
FEDER

Weatherman Triemstra to retire from WGN-AM

Roger Triemstra, meteorologist on Bob Collins' top-rated morning show, announced his retirement Thursday after 33 years of forecasts and folksy humor at WGN-AM (720).

Triemstra, who will deliver his farewell forecast June 26, said he plans to spend more time with his grandchildren and at his home in Michigan.

"Thirty-three years in this business is almost unheard of," Collins told Triemstra on the air Thursday. "It really has been a wonderful run. . . . Thanks for being a friend and thank you for being so much a part of this radio station."

Replacing Triemstra at WGN will be the around-the-clock services of the Weather Channel, a cable television network with a staff of more than 80 meteorologists.

"Roger talked to us about his retirement some time ago and was kind enough to allow us to find a suitable replacement before announcing his decision," said Mary June Rose, program director of WGN. "We'll miss him and his expertise greatly."

Triemstra, who served as a weather officer with the Air Force, began his broadcast career at WLS-Channel 7. He joined WGN-AM and WGN-Channel 9 in 1965. In 1982, he became full-time meteorologist for the radio station.

"I've had a lot of good times," Triemstra told listeners. "What I want to make sure of is, when I leave, I want to leave with me feeling good and with everybody else feeling good, and that's the way it's going to be."

Roger Triemstra
'Feeling good'

Triemstra's retirement closely follows those of WGN veterans Wally Phillips and Paul Rogers.

In 2018, I was honored to be inducted into the WGN Radio Walk of Fame, and was thrilled to have many of my former colleagues in attendance, including Anne Maxfield and Tracy Heuvelman.

It was a chilly day, so I was given a Blackhawks blanket to keep warm as the Class of 2018 posed with other Walk of Fame members.
Left to right: *Chuck Swirksy, Dave Eanet, Lyle Dean, Mary Van deVelde, Steve Bertrand, Dan Fabian, Judy Pielach, Bob Manewith (representing Pierre Andre), Anne Maxfield and David Kaplan. Seated next to me are Marilyn Miller, the longtime producer for Wally Phillips, and Orion Samuelson.*

Gerrie stands to be acknowledged after I introduced her during my speech.

Hot and Humid

The South Holland, Illinois, outlook for April 11, 1930, was probably something like: "Sunny, hot and humid. Midday temperatures near record highs. Cooler by the lake." As it turned out, the mercury topped out at 90. April days in the 90s are extremely rare in the Chicago area and have occurred on only four dates since 1871. Current Chicago climatologist Frank Wachowski said that in addition to back-to-back 90s in 1930, the city's only other occurrences were a pair of 91-degree highs recorded on April 30, 1942, and April 22, 1980. It must have been awfully uncomfortable for my mother. Besides being afflicted with pleurisy, she was giving birth to a future weatherman.

Lena (Leena) Van Drunen was 16 when she married my father, Jacob (Jakobus) Triemstra, who was two years older. Both were born in America, Lena on June 12, 1901, in South Holland to Rokus P. and Maartje (nee Vander Aa) Van Drunen; Jacob on August 31, 1898, in Roseland, Illinois, to Kornelius and Helena (Lentje) (nee Veltkamp) Triemstra. Jacob's parents were among the first waves of settlers who arrived in South Holland; both were born in Dongeradeel Municipality, Friesland, Netherlands. Lena's parents were American born, but her paternal grandparents, Pieter and Hendrica (nee De Graaff) Van Drunen were immigrants from Sleeuwijk, Werkendam Municipality, Noord-Brabant, Netherlands. Her maternal grandparents, Gerrit and Naatje (nee Ver Meulen) Vander Aa, were from Noordeloos, Giessenlanden Municipality, Zuid-Holland, Netherlands.

By the time I made an appearance, they already had four girls: 12-year-old Esther, 10-year-old Helen, 8-year-old Ruth, and 6-year-old Emily. The older three were thrilled with the arrival of their baby brother. Emily, though, didn't like that her privileged position as baby of the family had been usurped. She came around eventually, though, no doubt unable to resist my charm and wit. The doting I received from my sisters enabled

My maternal grandparents, Rokus and Maartje (Mary) Van Drunen.

My paternal grandparents, Kornelius and Helena (Lentje) (nee Veltkamp) Triemstra.

My childhood home in South Holland.

my becoming the rascal of the family, a position I eagerly accepted and aggressively carried with me into other parts of my life.

While my mother continued to fight the pleurisy she contracted during pregnancy, a nurse was brought in to help take care of me. She later became a relative after marrying my mother's cousin. Although not totally able to care for me, my mother absolutely smothered me with love. I could have set the house on fire, and she would've thrown gasoline on it so it would have been her fault.

As for my father, I believe he was relieved and thrilled to have another Y chromosome in the house. The two of us would often sneak off together to do guy things, later working with him at a steel mill, and helping him build houses. We had a wonderful relationship. Dad had a great sense of humor; it's probably where I got mine.

As its name would suggest, South Holland was settled by Dutch immigrants. There were a lot of surnames that began with "de," or "De," such as de Vries and De Graff, or names with consecutive vowels such as Paarlberg, Klaas and Walvoord, and names with both, such as de Groot. Walvoord was the name of the only doctor in South Holland when I was born, and I read that his standard charge for delivering a baby was $10. At that price, I'd say I was a bargain.

A 1936 photo of Dad and me.

Historical accounts say South Holland was settled by Dutch immigrant Hendrik DeJong. It has been spelled DeJonghe, de Jong, de Young and DeYoung through the years, and pronounced dee-YOUNG. He initially landed in Holland, Michigan, in

1846 with his wife and 13 children. But starting a farm there was out of the question because of the dense forests, so they packed up and sailed across Lake Michigan to the swampy lowlands similar to what they'd left behind in the Netherlands. At first, the settlement was called "de Laage Prairie," which translates to "the Low Prairie." That's not to be confused with another Dutch settlement about 10 miles north called "de Hooge Prairie," or "the High Prairie," which was later renamed Roseland. One of Roseland's notable products was another DeYoung, the musician Dennis.

The De Laage or the Low Prairie was named South Holland in 1870. The name was proposed by the Justice of the Peace at that time, Peter DeYoung. Today, it's known as the Village of South Holland, and the town's official website shows the motto as "Faith, Family, Future." When I was growing up, the future was a little fuzzy, but faith and family were crystal clear. I recall the water tower had a painting of a pair of praying hands and the slogan: "The community that prays." There was primarily one faith: Calvinist. There were about 2,900 residents when I was a boy and I'll bet 2,850 had a Dutch connection, and most were members of the Dutch Reformed Church, of which there were at least six in our little town.

As I understand it, the church was based on John Calvin's very conservative philosophy and strict rules against anything that would involve fun being had. Sunday was definitely not a fun day. My grandmother went to church morning, noon, and night on Sundays, and the rest of us were usually dragged along for some or all of it. Both of my parents were raised in the church and toed the line as children. The way my dad was raised, he would get up on Sunday morning, get dressed in his going-to-church clothes, and go to church in the morning, in the middle of the day, and at night. There was no playing outside, no riding bikes, no fun.

When it came to my turn, I passed the time counting the bricks on the wall or counting the pipes on the organ. Few things will discourage a child from becoming a follower than forcing them to sit in church three times a day. I am a believer, but I didn't buy into all the rules and restrictions. It was reading C.S. Lewis that informed me the most about Jesus Christ, not the Dutch Reformed Christian Church or its pastors. Known best for *Chronicles of Narnia*, Lewis wrote books arguing for the existence of God and examining the arguments of skeptics. *Mere Christianity, The Problem of Pain,* and *Miracles* were among the books that influenced me.

The conclusion of the American Civil War was marked with the beginning of a "Dutch Civil War" in the Reformed Church in South Holland. In 1865, a large number of Dutch families withdrew from the South Holland Reformed Church and established the True Dutch Reformed Church. The split came because of a feeling by many members that the church was becoming too "Americanized"— not in formal doctrine but in language, customs, and spirit. Later on, the name changed to Christian Reformed, the church that I attended throughout my life and still do today. The reasons cited for withdrawal from the other church were: departure from the standards for Calvinism, particularly in regard to the doctrine of election and atonement; neglect of catechism preaching and teaching; the use of hymns rather than psalms in church services; the toleration of Free Masons as members in good standing; private baptisms instead of regular baptismal services; open communication; neglect of family visiting as required for church order.

What saved my sisters and me from being raised under the thumb of strict Calvinists seven days a week was geography. We lived in the country and the Christian schools were in town. It wasn't easy or convenient for us to go to the Christian schools because they provided no bus service. And I give partial credit to my dad for allowing us to go to public schools. Because of the depression, he had to leave the farm and go to work in the steel mills where he was exposed to other people, other ways of life and other philosophies. I suppose he wanted us to experience a broader view of things.

I'm going to jump ahead for a moment as I haven't told you

ABOVE: *With my sister Ruth.*
BELOW: *I'm with Ruth (center) and Emily.*

about my wife, Gerrie. She was raised in the same strict Dutch Reformed Christian way, and Gerrie wanted our children to be raised the same way. Despite my misgivings, I went along with her to avoid conflict. That adherence to the old ways carried through until our youngest son was born, and then it all pretty much went out the window, as I appreciated other beliefs.

The church's impact on South Holland was significant. It was a dry town — no alcohol was sold — no businesses were open on Sundays. You couldn't really do anything.

South Holland then was solidly Republican. During the first election, a search was made to find a Democratic candidate. This was difficult because no one in the town was a Democrat. Finally, to comply with the belief in this country that a two-party system is essential, several men agreed to be Democrats for a day and the election was held.

South Holland also had onions. Lots and lots of onions. You could smell them in the breeze. It became known as the "Onion Capital of the World," and my nickname in grade school was "Onions." Here is an account shared by Mr. Gerrit Pals about life on an onion set farm in South Holland:

> *I was one of the men in the community who planted, cultivated, harvested, and marketed the crop which South Holland became famous for – the onion set. The product raised was called a "set" because that is what was done with it early the next season. This bulb, which was grown from seed, was "set" out in the fields and would develop into one of many varieties of onions. The set, which was approximately the size of a small marble when harvested, was forced to stay small by overcrowding the seeds in a row, and by harvesting them before they had a chance to develop.*
>
> *During the early years, when the onion set was grown in Ohio,*

Kentucky, and in the lower Lake Michigan area, the processes and steps in producing these onion sets were all done by hand. Rows were planted one-at-a-time, causing unevenness, and preventing machines from being used in them. Cultivation, or weeding between the rows, was done by means of wheel cultivators which were pushed by men if the ground was fairly soft and pulled and pushed by men if the ground was hard. Harvesting consisted of pulling the sets out by their tops, and either cutting or twisting these tops off by hand.

You could harvest about 60 bushels each on a good day; 40 in the morning and 20 in the afternoon. We would slow down after the sun got hot and we got tired from our morning harvesting races. After the sun became hot in the summer, the ground would get rock-hard, making weeding, cultivating, and harvesting an almost impossible job. The tops of the onion sets caused problems by themselves, either being too green and juicy or too dry and brittle. If the tops were green, there was no real problem for the farmer, but the workers would get the juice ground into their knees and clothes, causing everything including the Sunday morning service to smell like an onion patch. If the onion tops were too dry, harvesting was impossible because the tops would break off, and the set would be left in the hard ground. Most of the work was done by hand, giving the boys in the community a chance to work and earn a wage if they wanted to.

This was one of the jobs I did as a kid and earned a meager two cents a bushel. My sisters worked in the field right along beside me. The end of the season was celebrated with a cold slice of watermelon for each of us.

A lot of farmers made fortunes, but not my father. He was running a farm my mother's father, Grandpa Van Drunen, owned; in fact, we were living in one of the houses Grandpa built. He was a contractor and homebuilder and had built a big two-story home which my family rented for nine dollars a month. No indoor plumbing back then but eventually it was added to our home.

As I got a bit older, I began working as a laborer for various farmers in the South Holland area. That was hard work but not at all challenging, mentally. I figured out right away that being a laborer wasn't for me. I was the kind of kid who would take a clock apart to see what made it work. In our basement was a train set, and I couldn't afford to buy accessories like crossing gates and signal lights, so I cut up an old string of Christmas tree lights and made my own.

Farms back then were a lot different from the huge spreads we see today across the Corn Belt. Most were 10 to 20 acres, usually located just behind the houses that lined the roads. They were truck farms, raising a variety of vegetables to load on to wagons or trucks and take to markets and sell. When the Great Depression hit, coincidentally around the time of my birth, the farm couldn't support my family and Dad had to look for other work.

With little work to be found, we went on relief. Dad picked up whatever work he could. I suppose that's the root of my entrepreneurship, which played out later in life as I owned a roller-skating rink and a pizza place. When I was five or six, I'd go to the market to get food for women in the neighborhood, and they'd give me a couple of cents as a tip. At the end of the day, I might have earned a dime, and that was big money in those days. I also picked up vegetables that got left behind in farm fields — radishes, onions, carrots, and so on — and then sold them door to door for a couple of cents. Even as a little kid, I was always trying to see an opportunity to make a few bucks here and there.

It was a clannish community, a lot of people were related, and there was a lot of helping each other out. We were poor as church mice, but I had no idea. I don't remember wanting for anything, and my sisters spoiled me rotten. They were going to make sure their baby brother got what he needed.

My oldest sisters, Esther and Helen, were both married and living next door to us in a house our grandfather built, one couple upstairs, the other downstairs. They bought me a bright red car-wagon. I don't recall whether it was a Red Flyer, which were made in Chicago, but it could have been. I used it to carry the groceries to my "clients," but I didn't like the color. In those days, the Model T, as Henry Ford famously said, came in any color as long as it was black. So, I found some black paint and painted my wagon. I much preferred the black, but my mom made me use gasoline to scrub it back to its original color.

When President Roosevelt set up the WPA (Workers Progress

The car-wagon I painted black. I hated wearing knickers.

Administration) jobs program in 1935, there were 10 million unemployed men in the United States. Three million got WPA jobs and I'm thankful Dad was one of them. He was a life-long Republican and likely didn't give FDR the credit he was due for saving the country. I remember the day FDR died. I was 15 years old and cried like a baby.

Another entrepreneurial opportunity presented itself to me when WPA crews were building a new bridge over Thorn Creek at East 170th Street, replacing a wooden bridge with a concrete one. My mother would help me make a pail full of lemonade, and I'd put it in my wagon and pull it to the bridge, selling it to the thirsty workers for two cents a glass.

Having older sisters also paid off for me. When I was 11 or 12, I got a job washing and polishing cars at a gas station. I'd get 75 cents a wash and $1.25 for a polish. Three or four brothers owned the station and one of them, Johnny, was dating my oldest sister, Esther. It was a neighborhood hangout, and guys were always stopping in because they knew I had sisters and figured being nice to me might be a little bit of an in to getting a date with my sisters. It was all good until Esther broke up with Johnny. I guess he figured he'd get even with her through me. He told me he'd give me a quarter if I drank a bottle of 7-Up, smoked a cigar, and ran around the gas pumps 10 times. I should have known better. I made it home and collapsed on the front lawn. It was raining and I was so sick. My mother came out and I told her I had the quick flu. I never did tell her what happened because that would have caused a big brouhaha in the neighborhood because she would have raised Cain with the boys' mothers. I'll never forget that cigar. It said "King Edward, a mild smoke" on the wrapper.

When I was 10, I contracted rheumatic fever. I remember the doctor using a tape measure across my chest to diagnose my heart as being enlarged. I still have "AFib," atrial fibrillation, as a result of the rheumatic fever, but the illness didn't keep me from living an adventurous life — and a long one. I'm 91 as of this writing.

Schoolwork came easy to me. The first school I went to, McKinley

ABOVE: *The family, circa 1934.*
BELOW: *The family, years later.*

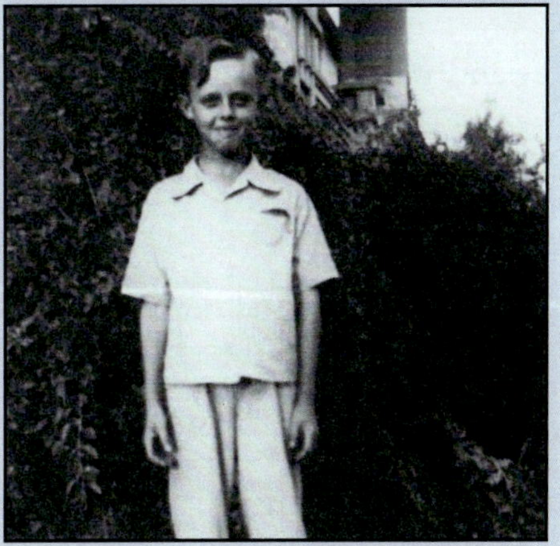
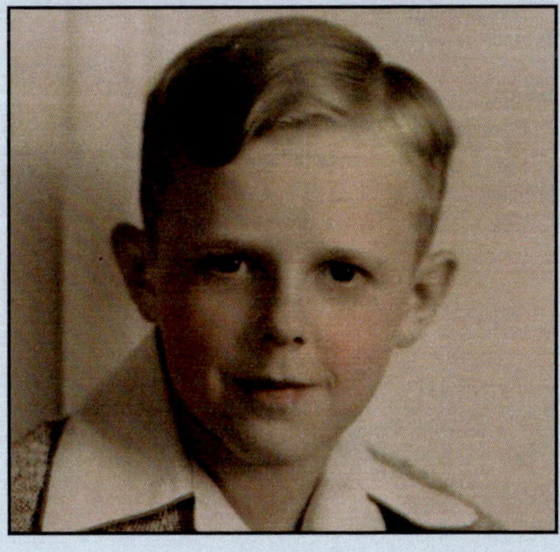

Photos from various times during my childhood.

Grade School, was a couple of miles away and a bus would pick us up in front of our house. The school was so small the first three grades were in the same room. Five boys and three girls. After I had made quick work of my first-grade lessons one day, I started doing the second-grade work. My teacher, Lillian Bruin, decided there was no reason I should waste my time in first grade and skipped me to second. That worked out well academically, but not so well socially. I was a little guy, and a favorite pastime of the schoolgirls was to chase me and beat me up. My academic prowess also resulted in boredom, which I eased by acting out. At least once that resulted in me getting kicked out of school. I didn't want my parents to know, so I walked home, hid in a ditch until the bus came by and walked into the house as if it were just another routine day after school.

I was always a fan of music and in grade school the band leader assigned me the trombone. I had no formal training, no lessons, in fact, I cannot read music. I played completely by ear and when I was older, I continued to play, including in the South Holland Community Band. On one occasion I played on WGN radio. And the tradition of trombone playing continued on: My two sons played the trombone and two of my grandsons play the trombone.

My graduating class of 1943 from McKinley Grade School.

The Vultures

What was unusual about my years at Thornton Township High School in Harvey was that I ran in different circles at the same time. I was an honor student and was fairly well liked by the same kinds of kids who did well academically and socially. But I didn't want to be known as an intellect.

I also didn't want to be viewed as a sissy. I was a runt who was the baby in the family with four sisters and there's no doubt it affected me psychologically. When I graduated from grade school, I had to stand on a box for the school photo and I was still the shortest one. That hadn't changed by the time I was a teenager, and I was not very athletic, at least not for the typical school sports like football. The kinds of athletics I got involved in had very little to do with my stature: ice skating and roller skating, for example.

So, I joined the Vultures, and they were exactly what you'd think they would be with a name like that: a bunch of roughnecks. I liked the idea of belonging to a group of tough guys who ignored the rules, followed their own path and lived on the edge. Clearly, as I'd find out quickly, it was not a good decision on my part.

My first taste of what life as a Vulture was going to be like was the initiation. They stripped me down and shaved my private parts. That was to humiliate me and send me a message: Don't mess with us or we'll cut your thing off. Message received.

Not surprisingly, I was the brightest guy in the group but that didn't stop me from doing some dumb things. One day in the fall, we ditched school to spend the day in Saugatuck, Michigan. There were seven of us in the car — three in front and four crammed in back — and when we left Harvey, I was sitting in the front. When we stopped for gas in Benton Harbor one of the guys in the back wanted to sit in the front, so I had to move to the back, and because it was so crowded another guy sat on my lap.

About 20 minutes later, we're going too fast — we're Vultures, always on the edge — and a car pulls out from a side road, and we hit him head on. The head of the Vulture who traded places with me went through the windshield, completely disfiguring his face. Because I was sheltered by the guy sitting on my lap, I was the only one who didn't go to the hospital. They put me on a Greyhound bus and sent me home.

I had to explain to my parents what I was doing in Benton Harbor when they thought I was in school. I tried to make up some excuse, but there was no talking my way out of that one. Then there was the school. The rest of the Vultures were expelled, but it didn't matter much because they were in the hospital and couldn't go to school. I, however, had to suffer the embarrassment of being dragged by my mom to the school for a meeting with the Dean of Boys, Fred Umbaugh, who oversaw school discipline. I expected to be put on detention for seven days, but he surprised me by being very gracious. He was gracious because I was an honor student, and he never liked that I was part of the Vultures group. He didn't expel me or put me on detention. All he wanted was for me to apologize, which I did.

In his wisdom, Mr. Umbaugh guided me to what I eventually figured out: compensating for my size by trying to be tough wasn't going to end well for me. God provided me with an above average brain and using it would carry me through life. I'm fortunate the Dean recognized that and helped me get on a better path.

My tenure with the Vultures ended, as did my association with those fellas. I did maintain lifelong friendships with other kids I grew up with and Gerrie and I shared quite some adventures with them and their spouses.

I may have no longer been a Vulture, but I was still a rascal and prankster. I still have a goofy side to me. People really don't know what to do with me, and I love it that way. If someone tries to put me in a box, I'll kick the sides out. I think God decided the world had to have one of these guys that's half nuts and he picked me.

God also picked Bob Dean for me. Bob and I met as freshmen in high school, and we became friends for life. In fact, he was the best man at my wedding. Bob was a prankster like me, and we did a lot of rascally stuff, some of which we shouldn't have. After finishing high school, we moved up a floor to Thornton Junior College. In chemistry class, Bob and I had been appointed fire marshals by a teacher who knew we were mischievous, but surely never thought we'd try to burn the chemistry lab down, which we almost did. The rest of the class left for a coffee break and left their Bunsen burners on low, heating some chemicals. Bob and I decided to see what would happen if we turned the burners up to high. There were some flammable reagents on the shelf above the burners, and the flames were so high the reagents started to combust. So, as fire marshals, we grabbed the fire extinguishers and sprayed the whole room down, making a huge mess. It was terrible. Bob and I were friends for many years, but he died quite young.

After two years of junior college, the Illinois Institute of Technology was my next stop. It was on 31st at State Street and I took the streetcar from South Holland. Until 1940, the school was called Armour Tech, established by the Armour Meat company family who donated the money to start an elite engineering school.

The Illinois Tech website describes the origin as being the result of a plea from the pulpit.

> *In 1890 when advanced education was often reserved for society's elite, Chicago minister Frank Wakeley Gunsaulus delivered what came to be known as the "million-dollar sermon." From the pulpit of his South Side church, near the site Illinois Institute of Technology now occupies, Gunsaulus said that with $1 million, he could build a school where students of all backgrounds could prepare for meaningful roles in a changing industrial society.*
>
> *Inspired by Gunsaulus's vision, Philip Danforth Armour Sr. (1832–1901) gave $1 million to found Armour Institute — and*

Armour, his wife, Malvina Belle Ogden Armour (1842–1927), and their son Jonathan Ogden Armour (1863–1927), continued to support the university in its early years. When Armour Institute opened in 1893, it offered professional courses in engineering, chemistry, architecture, and library science.

Illinois Tech was created in 1940 by the merger of Armour Institute and Lewis Institute. Located on the West Side of Chicago, Lewis Institute, established in 1895 by the estate of hardware merchant and investor Allen C. Lewis, offered liberal arts as well as science and engineering courses for both men and women. At separate meetings held by their respective boards on Oct. 26, 1939, the trustees of Armour and Lewis voted to merge the two colleges. A Cook County circuit court decision on April 23, 1940, solidified the merger.

Engineering classes suited me. I was an honor student, was in three honorary fraternities including Tau Beta Pi, the engineering equivalent of Phi Beta Kappa, and shed some of my rascalness; probably because I was too busy studying and working. I was what they called a co-op student, which meant I alternated academic studies with full-time jobs. I had to. IIT was an expensive school, but I was able to pay my way.

My off-semester job was with my dad at the Acme Steel mill in Whiting, Indiana. I would work in the plant for a semester, then go to school the next. That's why it took me three years to complete my last two years of college. Even while attending classes, I worked part time at Fred Nelson's Men's Store. Those off-semesters when I worked with my dad were memorable. We had always bonded as the only males in the family, but those times when we worked at Acme brought us closer. We took lunch breaks together, eating and talking about who knows what. It was special.

If you graduated from IIT, you were guaranteed a job. Engineers were in demand in the early '50s, and IIT had a reputation as one of the best schools in the country, right up there with MIT, Cal Tech or Case

Institute of Technology, which is now Case Western Reserve University. And I graduated with all sorts of honors and awards, so I knew there would be a lot of offers.

My graduation was a big deal in the family. I was the first of my immediate family to graduate from college and I think I was the first in the whole extended family. You can imagine how proud my mother felt. Here's that boy she babied his whole life and put up with his shenanigans, and he graduates with honors. I know Dad was proud, too, because he saw it as a way for me to have a better life than he'd had.

My dad, Jacob (Jakobus) Triemstra.

LEFT: *My Thornton Township High School graduation photo.*
RIGHT: *My Illinois Institute of Technology graduation photo.*

Graduation from Thornton Junior College.

The nurse who cared for me as a child when my mom was ill. She later married into our extended family.

Mom and Dad on their 50th anniversary.

With my sisters Emily and Helen.

My sisters and their husbands: Harry and Esther Lagestee, Ed and Helen Klompmaker, George and Ruth Daehn, Mike and Emily Van Zuidam, and Gerrie and me.

Clowning around with my sisters.

Nephews Jay Klompmaker, Terry Van Zuidam, Dan Lagestee and brother-in-law Mike Van Zuidam.

N
W
E
S

The Shoe

When Geraldine Porter entered my life

Being a bit of a rascal worked to my advantage in the dating game. In those days, girls liked boys who were a little on the wild side. I had plenty of dates in high school, but the love of my life entered the picture on the Fourth of July 1947 at Wicker Park in Highland, Indiana. It was a big picnic with a carnival. Lots of families and extended families were there, all the aunts and uncles and cousins. I'm standing with a couple of buddies watching a ride called the Chair-O-Plane. You sit on a chair that's attached to a chain, and it goes up and down and swings around and around. We get in line and while we're waiting, a shoe lands right in front of me. I picked it up, looked around, and did what any mischievous rascal would do: I tossed it up into a tree. It lodged in a little crook between branches.

A couple of my girl cousins who'd been on the ride, Marilyn Van Der Zee and Doris Van Der Aa, came running up to me and said, "What did you do with that shoe?" I pointed up at the tree. "Why did you do that?" one of them demanded. "Well," I told her, "I'm standing here watching you guys, minding my own business, and I could have been killed by that shoe coming down, so I threw it up in the tree."

The shoe belonged to a classmate at the school they attended, Highland Christian School. My cousin said, "What are you going to do now?" The owner of the shoe was standing with them, and I said, "Would you give me your other shoe?"

She did and I threw it into the tree, knocked the other one loose and they both came down. I handed her the shoes and said, "You know, there are fireworks here tonight. Would you like to stay and watch them with me?" And that's how I met Geraldine Porter, the girl who would be my wife for over seven decades.

Baby Geraldine

Gerrie with her dad, left, and two hired hands on the Porter truck farm.
Below: Pitching in with the farm work.

ABOVE AND BELOW LEFT: *Gerrie as a young girl. Little did she know as she donned the umbrella that there would be a meteorologist in her life.*
BELOW RIGHT: *A late in life photo of Mom and Dad Porter.*

ABOVE: *Gerrie as a young girl.* BELOW: *Gerrie's high school graduation picture, and wearing her honeymoon suit purchased at Morris B. Sachs.*

We didn't start dating right away, though. I was starting college that fall and she was starting high school, so I thought she was a little young. I was 17 and she was 14. And I didn't call her. Weeks went by and she wrote me a letter, asking if she'd done something wrong because I hadn't called her. She wrote, "If I did, I want to apologize." This letter touched me, and I knew that this girl was special, and I wanted her in my life. What a sweet person. No other girl I had dated showed either this sweetness for me or appreciation of me.

Labor Day was our first date. We went to Michigan City for a festival and had silhouettes cut out of our face profiles, which to this day are hanging in my bedroom. We had a lot of fun dates and since it was a "sin" to attend movies, we found other things. We went roller skating, to the Indiana beach, to parades and festivals and to stock car and midget car races.

Johanna and Herman Porter, circa 1953.

Gerrie's parents were Herman and Johanna Porter. Herman was a truck farmer, meaning during growing season he'd load up a truck of produce and drive it to the Chicago market. Gerrie had a sister 12 years older, Petronella, who was born on August 6, 1921, and a younger brother, Norman, six years younger born November 28, 1939. He was a real rascal and rebelled against his dad and the old, strict, Calvinistic ways. Once we were married, we became close friends with Gerrie's brother and sister and their spouses; we went on numerous vacations with them and thoroughly enjoyed their company.

Gerrie's mother was an angel and took a liking to me from the start, mainly because she knew my aunt Alice Van Drunen, quite well. This was my mom's brother's wife, my aunt whose son was killed on a bicycle. He was hitching a ride on the back of a car. He let go of the car and ran into a telephone pole. From the time that happened, I was kind of a replacement for her son.

After I met Gerrie's mother, I thought to myself, what a wonderful grandmother she would be for my children. And she was. My kids remember her as a wonderful grandmother, but she was more of a disciplinarian than Grandpa Porter. He let them get away with much more and introduced them to facets of life their grandma surely would not have approved. My daughter Cheri remembers her grandpa sticking the grandkids in his truck to go to the pickle factory and slipping a little pinch of chew in each of their lips!

Gerrie and I never became an exclusive couple. We both continued to date other people. I would date "Philistines," girls that I would take to parties but never would have married and then I would take Gerrie to church events, weddings, and other respectable social gatherings. She was the "marrying type" and I knew in my heart she was the one. Gerrie was a patient woman, but she had her limits, too. Gerrie and I met in 1947 and come 1952 we were still dating. She was getting impatient with me, but her mother told her, "Don't let him get away. That kid's got some future." I got the message and on April 11, my birthday and Good Friday night, I popped the question. Kind of. As Christians, our families were all headed for church, and I was at the Porter house, planning to attend church with Gerrie and the family. I was standing by the doorway of her bedroom and when she came out, I handed her a box. She opened it up and there was an engagement ring. She said, "What's this?" I said, "What does it look like?" Not very romantic, I have to admit. We headed out to church, and she spent most of the service with her arm resting on the back of the church pew so the church attendees could see her new ring and they would know she was officially engaged.

My sister Ruth and her husband, George, owned Daehn's Jewelry in South Holland and Ruth helped me decide on a ring for Gerrie. I needed the help and really appreciated my sister's guidance. Gerrie and I were busy planning the wedding and my mom was getting too involved in the planning process and decision making, and it was adding to Gerrie's stress since we didn't want to have a long engagement. After all, I was in St. Louis, and she wanted to join me there.

Gerrie wanted to have a bigger life than what she had on the farm. She started planning the wedding and I was fine with any of her decisions, so I stayed out of the planning stage. As was the custom then, we would get married at Gerrie's church in Highland, Indiana, and have the reception there, too. My mom didn't like the idea of having the reception at the church. She wanted to have the reception at Calvin Christian School in South Holland, which was the school located in her backyard. This made no sense to have a reception an hour away from the church and have the guests drive there in the harsh winter weather.

All the conflict with my mom brought Gerrie to tears and she returned her engagement ring to me. She could not see a life with me when it was already starting out with so much tension and disagreements with my mom. We had a long talk and I convinced her that once we were married, we could get away from all the drama and we would have our own life, starting with moving out of the area to St. Louis. I told her that I didn't want to leave the house without her having the ring back on her finger. She slipped it on and continued to plan our wedding.

Gerrie's engagement ring was beautiful and a single solitary diamond; but I wanted more for her and to show her I truly would be there for her and how much I loved her. I took her ring and brought it back to my sister's jewelry store and she designed a circle of diamonds that she could slide in around her solitary ring. She had the option of wearing just the solitary or adding the circle of diamonds around it. But she left the circle of diamonds on; she loved the ring, and I so appreciated the beautiful design that my sister Ruth created. She significantly cut the cost for me, knowing I was living on a military salary, and her kindness was not forgotten.

Mom got her way with the reception, though. The wedding was on a Friday night January 23, 1953, in Highland, Indiana, and the reception was in South Holland. It was cold, about 37 degrees, but luckily there was no snow coming down. Gerrie wanted a colorful, celebratory reception since it was right after the New Year and it was just that: Purple, red and pink were the colors. Here's the wedding announcement in the local newspaper:

Roger Triemstra Takes Indiana Girl as Bride

The Highland Christian Reformed Church was the scene of a beautiful wedding on Friday at 7:00 p.m., when Geraldine Porter, daughter of Mr. and Mrs. Herman Porter of Gary, Indiana, became the bride of Roger Lee Triemstra, son of Mr. and Mrs. Jacob Triemstra, Park Plaza, South Holland. Rev. Edward F. Visser officiated at the double ring ceremony. Mr. Porter gave his daughter in marriage before an altar decorated with baskets of white gladiolus and chrysanthemums.

The bride wore a lovely white slipper satin gown with a lace bodice and nylon tulle over skirt. Her fingertip veil was held in place with a nylon tulle headpiece piped with satin. She carried a white Bible covered with a white orchid and streamers of stephanotis.

Petronella Kuiper attended her sister as matron of honor wearing a gown with purple velveteen bodice and orchid net skirt and a matching purple velveteen hat. She carried a bouquet of white orchid chrysanthemums on a purple velveteen muff. Ruth Scheeringa and Ella Joan Schoon wore identical styled gowns to the matron of honor in American red and pink net skirt with matching hats. They carried bouquets of white and pink chrysanthemums on American red beauty muffs. Gay Lee Klompmaker, niece of the bridegroom, was flower girl wearing American beauty red gown fashioned after the bridesmaids with matching hat. She carried a basket of pink and white chrysanthemums.

Robert Dean served the bridegroom as best man, and Michael Van Zuidam and George Daehn were groomsmen. Dick Kuiper and Harry Lagestee assisted as ushers. Rick Kuiper, nephew of the bride, was ring bearer.

Mrs. Porter wore a navy dress trimmed in pink with pink and navy accessories. The mother of the bridegroom was attired in a navy dress with white trim and navy accessories.

Mrs. Roland Arnell sang "At Dawning", "God Sent You To Me," and "Savior Like a Shepherd Lead Us" accompanied by Andrew Vogel at the organ. The couple greeted their guests at a reception held at Calvin Christian School in South Holland at 8:30 p.m. Out-of-town guests came from Grand Rapids, Michigan.

The bride is a graduate of the Illiana Christian High school and was employed as a bookkeeper at the Northern Indiana Public Service company in Hammond, Indiana prior to her marriage.

The bridegroom is a graduate of the Thornton Township High school and the Illinois Institute of Technology. He was employed as an inspection engineer at the Standard Oil company before entering the service. He is now a Second Lieutenant in the Air Force and stationed in St. Louis, where he is training to be a weather officer.

The couple will reside in St. Louis.

BELOW, LEFT TO RIGHT: *Ella Joan Schoon, Ruth Scheeringa, Petronella Kuiper, the newlyweds, Robert Dean, George Daehn, and Michael Van Zuidam.*
FRONT: *Flower girl Gay Lee Klompmaker and ring bearer Rick Kuiper.*

LEFT TO RIGHT: *Jacob and Lena Triemstra, the newlyweds, and Johanna and Herman Porter.*

We had one night in Chicago in a nice hotel, and the next morning we got in our car and headed for St. Louis. On the way south, we stopped in Springfield and visited Lincoln's Tomb. It was tradition to rub and kiss Lincoln's brass nose for good luck. We did and we were on our way.

As they say, some marry up, some marry down. I married way above my level, and I made sure Gerrie knew it.

Gerrie was a terrific mother and loved caring for our children, enjoyed working in the home, and entertained quite a bit with relatives coming from the Chicago area to visit. She was a very good woman. But she trusted me and knew that any decisions I made about my career, or about our family, would always be in her best interest – she was my number one priority. "Rog, if you think that's what's best..." was her typical response.

One of those moments was after we'd moved back from Ohio. We were still living in that little trailer with Patti. One evening when Gerrie was at church, I was driving around with Patti and saw a "Homes for Sale" sign in Thornton, Illinois. I stopped, looked at the model home,

Gerrie was pregnant with Patti in this 1953 photo by our 26-foot trailer at the Ohio trailer park where we lived while I was stationed at Lockbourne AFB.

Little Patti and Gerrie in 1954.

and put money down on one. When Gerrie got back from church, I told her, "Honey, while you were at church, I went out and got a home." She replied, "Rog, if that's what you think's best..." We lived in that house for 10 years.

In that house, two more children would be born in our family: a son, Carl, and a daughter, Cheryl (Cheri). They were only about 18 months apart. Another son, Dean, was a "surprise," arriving eight years after Cheri was born. I remember when Gerrie told me she was pregnant. I had quite the inappropriate response, saying, "Are you kidding me?! We have to go through all of that baby stuff again!?" But Dean came along and enjoyed a more relaxed upbringing than our other children.

Above and below: *Carl, Patti, and Cheri.*

Our "surprise," Dean, in 1969 and 1970.

I was always called "Rog" by Gerrie; she never had pet names for me like honey or sweetheart. "Roger," though, is what she called me if she wasn't happy with me. Generally, just a look from her was all it took. Gerrie was very tolerant of my nonsense, but even she had her limits.

Gerrie was more adventuresome than most people knew her to be and she and I traveled the world. We also shared many hobbies: snow skiing, snowmobiling, RV road trips and some water sports, but she was never a big fan of water and she tolerated boat rides for our children. She was also funny. When people would say to her, "How do you put up with that guy?" she would say, "Well, we never talk divorce. Murder, yes, but not divorce."

We were madly in love and marrying her was the greatest thing that ever happened to me. Gerrie is not specifically mentioned in every one of my stories throughout this book. It is not necessary — she was ever-present, my true partner in life, we truly shared this life together. We were Rog and Gerrie, simple as that. So just know that if my story is being told, so is hers.

The Brats

Gerrie was part of a group of girls attending Illiana Christian High School who became known as "The Brats." They'd been friends since grammar school and were smart and attractive, which the senior boys took notice of when the girls entered the freshman class. The senior girls, not liking that these freshmen girls were stealing their boyfriends started calling them "The Brats." They remained friends throughout their lives. Two of them were my cousins.

"The Brats" at Indiana Dunes. That's Gerrie on top.
BELOW LEFT: *A 1994 reunion of The Brats and cousins.*
BELOW RIGHT: *The Brats in 2002.*

Our first home without wheels in Thornton, Illinois.

Gerrie and I with Patti, Cheri and Carl at our home in Thornton.

Gerrie with her older sister Petronella and younger brother Norman.

Left to right: Petronella, me, Gerrie, Norman and his wife Barb. I got along really well with all of Gerrie's family, but her brother Norman and I were buddies. We got along great. He was a self-taught contractor, building all sorts of commercial buildings and apartment buildings; a hard worker and just a wonderful guy.

Gerrie was a great dresser, always very stylishly with nothing overlooked. Her mother was a seamstress, and Gerrie learned that from her. Back in the '30s and '40s when she was growing up, it was common for Johanna, Gerrie's mom, to work in the fields, picking radishes and onions. The daughters were left at home to do the cleaning and cooking and care for little Norman, but by that time Petronella, who was about 12 years older, had eloped with her boyfriend, Dick Kuiper. It was Gerrie's responsibility to help keep the house and watch Norman, and she became very good at that. She learned how to run a house at a very young age and was anxious to leave the farm to run her own home. She didn't hate the farm, but there was no way she was going to be a farm wife. And, other than horses, she wasn't a big fan of animals. We tried a dog or two when the kids were young and they begged for one, but they quickly wound up living at the Porter farm.

Meeting Gerrie, you wouldn't think she was up for new experiences or was very daring. She was more sedate and had a classy demeanor about her. You wouldn't picture her venturing out in a rubber raft to see penguins in Antarctica, or trekking deep into the Amazon, or hot air ballooning. But she loved it all and we had many fun times. We were great companions, and I guess the best way to sum up Gerrie and me is if you saw Gerrie, usually you saw me, and if you saw me, usually you saw Gerrie.

Her final days were with me, as a couple. Our daughter, Cheri, shares her observations.

> *"It was a true love story and I witnessed it firsthand in the last month or so of my mom's life. You don't really view your parents as anything more than just your parents; for sure, not two people who love each other. My dad did not want my mom placed in any other care facility, so 24-hour care was brought in to help him care for her. He wanted to be by her side and take care of her the best he could. They would sit on the couch, and she would fall asleep on his*

shoulder. In the morning when the caretakers would help her out of the bedroom, she would say to my dad, 'Well, there you are. I was looking everywhere for you!' We had hospice set up in the condo, but my mom never slept in any other bed but hers, lying next to my dad where she took her last breath."

Gerrie found this Vulture and I found Mother Teresa. She was that kind of a person, and if you knew her, you had to love her.

We had 73 of the most wonderful years together. Gerrie died on September 29, 2020. I miss her every day.

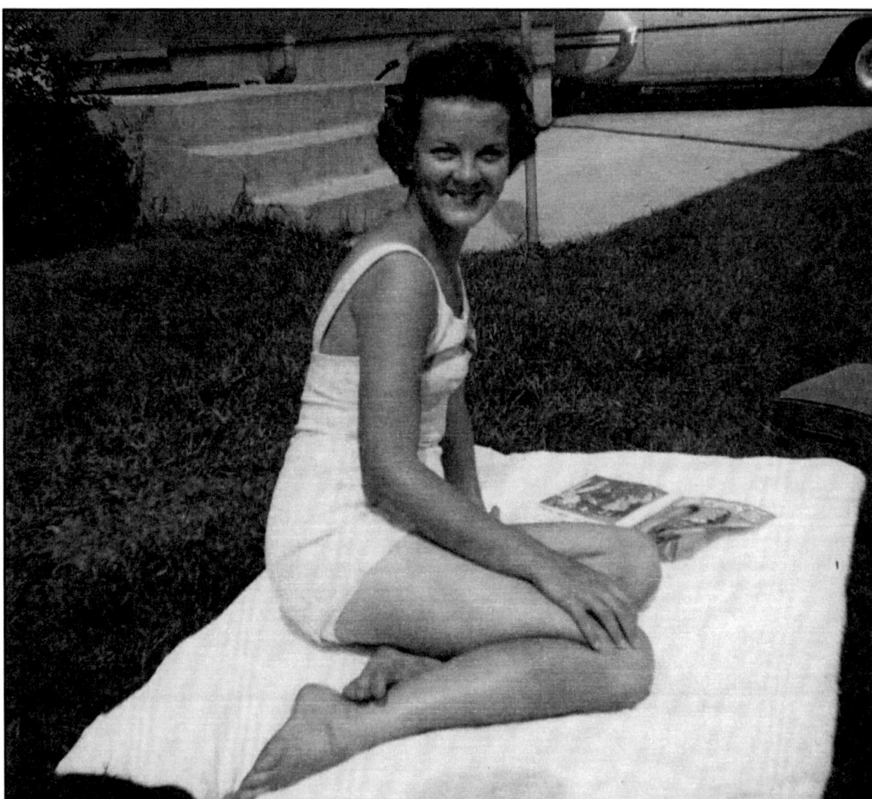

Gerrie catching some rays at our home in Thornton.
As you can see in the next group of photos, she loved the outdoors.

Kayaking at Silver Lake.

Swimming at Magen's Bay in St. Thomas, Virgin Islands.

Showing off her catch of the day.

Pet and Gerrie with their mother, Johanna Porter.

Gerrie's sister Pet and her husband, Dick Kuiper.

Pet, Norman and Gerrie

Gerrie and her sister Pet on Pet's 98th birthday.

Our 50th wedding anniversary was held at our son's house. We delayed it until summer because it was too cold in January for a pool party.

Gerrie and I enjoyed wonderful years of raising our family in this home in South Holland.

Christianity was a constant and positive presence in our lives. Here, we're singing with the other guests attending my grandson's wedding.

N
W
E
S

Opportunity

"Find a need and fill it."
— *Henry J. Kaiser*

"Find an opportunity and take it."
— *Roger L. Triemstra*

My awareness of meteorology began with the stink factory. That's what we called the rendering plant where dead animals from zoos and farms would be taken to be recycled. That's the polite way to put it. The process created a terrible odor, which we would smell in South Holland when the wind came out of the northeast. And when the wind came from the north or northwest, we could smell the Union Stockyards in Chicago. Luckily, prevailing winds are out of the southwest and west, so we didn't smell the odors very often.

Working on farms, I realized the importance of weather to farmers, and how nature gave signals of what was to come. On hot and sweaty days when the wind shifted and I could smell the lake, I knew that was good news because it would at least be cooler in the fields and, even better, rain was coming and I'd get the day off.

When I got to high school, I took a course in basic meteorology and I enjoyed it. I learned what a tremendous impact Lake Michigan had in determining the weather, not only in South Holland and Chicago, but for the surrounding region. There was a weather exhibit at the Museum of Science and Industry in Chicago that had a teletype machine typing out all the weather data and that caught my interest. I didn't study meteorology in college, but engineering and meteorology are similar — it's all math and physics.

The Korean War (June 25, 1950 — July 27, 1953) was on and the Air Force was looking for the best and brightest to join up. I registered for the draft when I turned 18. The draft was taking a lot of my friends and classmates into the Army, several of whom were injured and killed. My draft number came up and when I received the call, I explained that I had rheumatic fever as a child. The Army wasn't going to take my word for it, and sent me to Great Lakes Training Base for three days of evaluations. I left Great Lakes with no further information on my qualifications to join the Army or if I was going to be drafted.

I was in my graduate year at Illinois Institute of Technology in 1952, and there was a tremendous need for engineers and companies like Standard Oil and IBM were on campus recruiting. I had already accepted an offer from Standard Oil as a research engineer for the Amoco chemical division. But the U.S. Air Force was also among those recruiting and approached me. The Air Force made me this offer: "If you would be willing to go to graduate school and study meteorology, we'll make you an officer right away. In return, you'll spend three years on active duty as a weather officer." The Air Force did not need the findings from my evaluations from Great Lakes — this was not going to be a physically demanding position.

I had a life changing decision to make. Before I knew whether I'd flunked the physical, an Air Force captain, holding my officer's commission in his hand, told me I needed to take the oath to make it official. I told him, "Captain, you've got to understand that I just came from three days of exams. I don't know if they're going to reject me or send me off to boot camp." I think this offended him; he was career military, and I was sounding like a draft-dodger to him. He dropped my commission on the floor, put his boot on it, and said — and I remember it so clearly — "Young man, I've got one question. Are you willing to serve your country, or do I tear up the commission and you go home and see what happens?" "Well," I told him, "the way you put it, I'll serve the country." So, I took the offer. One day I'm a civilian, the next day I'm an officer in the Air Force headed for graduate school.

A few days later I received the letter in the mail from the Army with the results from my evaluation. I was 4-F, identifying me as unfit for military service. I panicked and tried to figure out how to undo my acceptance into the Air Force. It was really the first time in my life that a voice inside me said, "Rog, God has thrown you someplace and you're trying everything in your power to get out of it, but I want you to go and serve." I did, and it completely changed my life; one of the first instances in my life where I decided to go where an opportunity presented itself.

When my mom heard what I did she bawled like a baby. She thought it was awful, and couldn't believe I didn't try to stay out of the service. I told her not to worry about it, that I'd be fine; but I was her baby, after all. For me, it was an opportunity. Gerrie and I were both happy about my decision because she saw it as a future off the farm and I saw it as a challenge and an adventure to start my career path and my future outside of the confines of my South Holland life.

After graduate school, the guys I was with — actually, not all guys, there were three women — maybe 20 of us, all honor students with engineering degrees, were ready to go into the field and work as weather forecasters at an air base. But the Air Force realized none of us had any military training. Some of us didn't even know how to put on our uniforms. They sent us to San Antonio for basic training. Boot camp. It was frustrating for the training officers because they were all career guys and were used to bossing cadets around, not officers who had no interest in getting up at dawn to learn basic war skills or do military drills.

A captain with ribbons all over his uniform from his tours in World War II tried to teach us how to march in formation. We didn't have a clue. He did his best to intimidate us by walking behind us and kicking stones under our shoes hoping to trip us up.

One day, we stopped marching. "Captain," we told him, "we

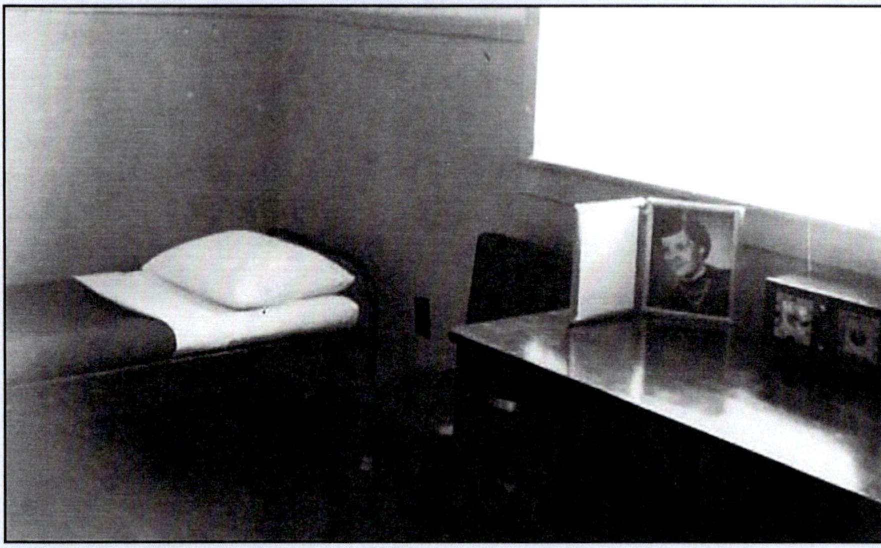

I sent this photo to Gerrie from basic training in San Antonio with the description on the back.

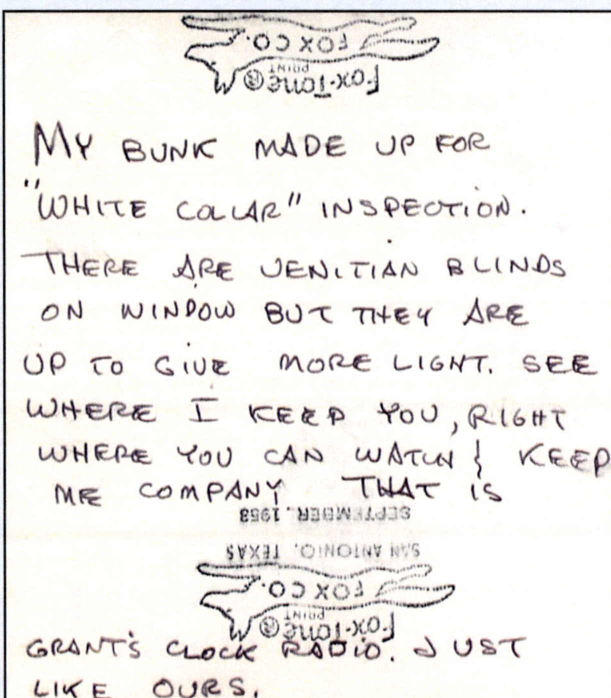

MY BUNK MADE UP FOR "WHITE COLLAR" INSPECTION. THERE ARE VENITIAN BLINDS ON WINDOW BUT THEY ARE UP TO GIVE MORE LIGHT. SEE WHERE I KEEP YOU, RIGHT WHERE YOU CAN WATCH & KEEP ME COMPANY THAT IS

SEPTEMBER, 1953
SAN ANTONIO, TEXAS

GRANT'S CLOCK RADIO. JUST LIKE OURS.

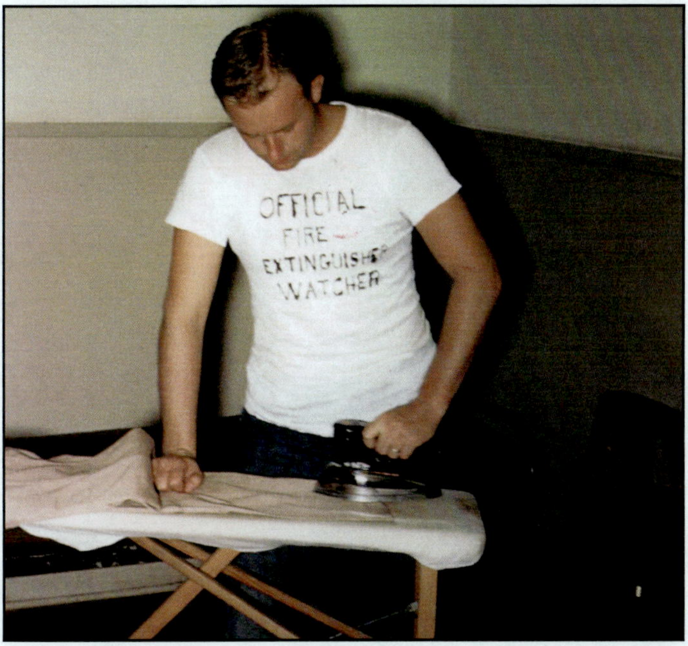

Ironing my uniform as "Official Fire Extinguisher Watcher."

need to talk with you. None of us are here because we want to be. We're here for one reason. We didn't want to get killed in Korea. We've all seen classmates of ours from high school and college come home in coffins."

The captain filed a complaint against us and when we were questioned about our actions, we were told not to worry about it.

Graduate school was at St. Louis University, a wonderful school. And a Jesuit school. There was no messing around in a Jesuit school. It was good for all of us young, smart punks. They handled us with kindness, but also with strictness.

St. Louis was a great place if you were young and single. There were good restaurants and baseball games with both the Cardinals and the Brownies there at that time. But I wasn't "single" — I would board the Illinois Central Railroad every weekend and go home to see Gerrie. I'd work at the men's store on Saturdays to make enough money to pay

my expenses and take Gerrie out. We had a great romance, but she felt very bad when I had to leave to go back to St. Louis. That led to us getting married sooner than we probably would have. Our wedding was in January of 1953, and Gerrie moved to St. Louis to spend the rest of graduate school with me.

After finishing, the plan was for me to go overseas to work for the Strategic Air Command but a couple of days before my group was scheduled to leave for France, I got sick. They put me in the military hospital and thought it might be a re-occurrence of rheumatic fever. That canceled my trip and changed the Air Force's plans for me. Instead of France, I got Ohio. Once I was given the all clear, I was assigned to Lockbourne Air Force Base near Columbus, Ohio. It was my job to brief pilots before they took off. These were mostly veterans, officers at least in their 30s, maybe 40s. I had to sign off on their clearance and would tell them if there was any weather they needed to be aware of. I was only 22

On the job in the Lockbourne Air Force Base weather office.

and should have been intimidated but for some reason, I was comfortable talking with any of them including legendary General Curtis LeMay, who I briefed a couple of times.

This was in the early years of the Cold War with the Soviets, and I had a radio hookup in my weather office where I could talk to these pilots anywhere in the world, including over the Arctic where they patrolled with atomic bombs loaded, ready to use. At that time, we refueled the bombers in the air and I'd give them a spot where the weather was good for them to refuel. I was their connection to home, and I developed some good friendships. They knew if they called me, I'd do anything I could for them because they were keeping us out of war. And at times the pilots needed a little down time to unwind after flying over the frigid North Pole. They'd radio as they were flying back and ask, "Tell me, how's the weather there?" I knew that meant they did not want to land at Lockbourne, so I'd tell them it was unsafe to land. They'd ask, "Well, where can we go?" I knew where they wanted to go. They wanted to land at either MacDill Air

ABOVE: *Gerrie at the door of our 26-foot home in Ohio.*
BELOW: *Gerrie was pregnant with Patti in this photo from 1953.*

ABOVE: *Holding Patti at the Ohio trailer park in 1954.*

Force Base in Tampa or at a base in Arizona and enjoy the warmth.

We had an officer's club with a swimming pool and one of the jobs of the duty officer, the weather officer, was to call the officer's club and get the wives out of the pool when storms were approaching. One day we had a major storm moving in and my priority was to get the warnings out and get the planes in the air and away from the storm avoiding potential damage on the ground. A typhoon had just hit Saipan and we lost 40 or so planes because they received no warnings to evacuate the base. I didn't want that to happen on my watch at Lockbourne.

I'm talking with a meteorologist at Wright-Patterson Air Force Base in Dayton when the commanding officer of Lockbourne, a colonel, calls. He said, "Lieutenant, there's a big storm coming in and I can see you haven't called to warn me about this so I can get the wives out of the pool." I said, "Colonel, I've got a whole bunch of planes here and my job is to protect the planes and the pilots. My concern is not the wives in the pool at the officers' club!" And a few other choice words...

I was going crazy and didn't know which way to turn to get all the warnings out. After the storm passed, I was summoned to the base commander's office. "Colonel, I understand you want to see me." He said, "Get in a brace," which means to stand at attention, very straight. He said, "And when you talk to me, keep in mind you're a lieutenant and I'm a colonel." I said, "Yeah, I know how all this crap works." He proceeded to chew me out and I informed him I was ready to leave anytime he wanted to let me go. "I have a good job waiting for me back home. In fact, I'll be making more money than I'm making here. If you want, I could be out of this town by midnight."

He said he was going to write me up, that I wasn't good military material. I wasn't having it and told him, "You'll hear more from me," and left the office. I went and talked to three of the SAC pilots who loved me for the reasons stated previously and one of them, a wing commander, told me, "Stormy, don't worry about it. Tell him to jump in a lake. I'll make sure it's all taken care of." This was a general who also flew and knew my work was important for the pilots, not the wives at the officer's club. He and two other officers wrote glowing reports about me, and the issue was resolved.

I was based at Lockbourne all three of the years I'd agreed to. Gerrie and I lived in a 26-foot trailer we'd pulled from South Holland and parked in a trailer park where other Air Force folks lived. That trailer was the source of a real sore spot for me. There was a great division of wealth in South Holland with the rich and powerful controlling most businesses, including the banks. When I went to the South Holland bank to get a small loan to buy the trailer, the banker turned me down. The banker, a guy I'll never forget, Milt Waterman, said I was a poor risk because I was going into the Air Force and it could be difficult for them to collect payments. I was furious. I'd lived there my entire life, my family had been there forever and had a good reputation. I had a degree in engineering and I was a second lieutenant in the Air Force. I was very upset. He said, "Well, we have a certain way we do things." I told him, "Your way is stupid." I went to another bank in Dolton and walked out with a check. It was ridiculous. And it cost my hometown bank a good customer. All of my personal and business banking was done through the Dolton bank moving forward.

We found a community in the trailer park and had a lot of fun together. We were all in the same boat. We found a church we liked and we really enjoyed living in Ohio. We even considered moving there after I was out of the service. Gerrie developed some close friends in the trailer park with the other weather officers' wives. They used to hang out their wash to dry on the clothesline and the other women followed suit — thinking that the weather officers' wives would surely know if it was going to rain. Little did they know that they had no clue either — they didn't consult their husbands before hanging out the wash.

It's also where our first child, Patricia Lynn, was born in 1954. When Gerrie's water broke, I took her to the base hospital, but didn't know what to do with myself or where to go. So, I went in the back door of the hospital and someone asked me what I was there for. I said, "My wife's water broke. I don't know what I'm supposed to do but I know she's going to have a baby, so we've got to take care of her." Lockbourne was close enough to home — only a six-hour drive — that our parents came out often to see us and our newborn little girl. Gerrie's mother, Mom Porter, came and stayed with us a while to help with the baby.

Gerrie was a great seamstress and she made all the curtains for the trailer. She sewed all the clothes for Patti and for herself. It was a great help living off a military salary

When my three years were up, the Air Force wanted me to stay on as a captain. I said, "You know what? I've enjoyed being in the service. It's given me a sense of pride being able to serve my country." Which was all true, but I didn't like the B.S. that's part of the military. Gerrie liked it there, but she'd always say — and I don't care what it was about — "Well, Rog, if you think that's the thing that we should do as a couple, go ahead."

We hooked up our trailer and drove home. At first, we parked the trailer in front of my parents' house until we could find a trailer park. We had turned the back of the trailer, the bedroom, into Patti's nursery, and

After returning to Standard Oil and Amoco Chemical from the service in 1956, I continued my work as a research and design engineer.

Gerrie and I slept on a hide-a-bed up front.

We got situated in a trailer park and at some point, we wanted to get a babysitter. Someone suggested a woman who lived in the park near us. Of course, I needed to do a little background check on her and it turned out she was a stripper. We continued our search for a more appropriate caregiver.

My job at Standard Oil and Amoco Chemical was waiting for me when I got back and I stayed there, earning 10 years: four years of credit while serving in the USAF and six years of employment. I also went back to IIT and got my MBA and taught a course in economics there.

One of the guys I worked with at Amoco Chemical received an offer from Kaiser Aluminum because Kaiser wanted to start a chemical division. I left Amoco to start work at Kaiser and became the manager of customer service and distribution. That was in Dolton, and I oversaw plants in New Jersey and California, too. I also supervised the building of a new laboratory, a distribution center, bought trucks and took care of all the things you take care of when you're starting a company. We were making chemicals that were under pressure. A lot of them were used in aerosol cans and they were used as refrigerants, so you had to have special equipment to handle it.

Kaiser sent me to Chile to look at the sheep that were going blind. The ozone layer wasn't protecting their eyes from the sun's rays. At that time, there wasn't a lot known about it. But aerosol sprays, containing a chemical made by Kaiser, were contributing to the ozone depletion worldwide, and it just happened to be a little worse in Chile because of its location close to Antarctica and the sun's radiation was stronger there.

Back here at home, we were seeing the problem in beauty parlors where large amounts of aerosol sprays were used in a confined space. The chemical in the spray was encountering the high temperatures in the parlor's furnaces and ventilation and was eating holes in the equipment. Kaiser put me on a task force with employees from DuPont, Union Carbide and a couple of other companies to study what was occurring. They knew

Channel 9 weekend weatherman Roger Triemstra reports to Chicago viewers in a straightforward, just-plain-folks manner. During the week, he's chief engineer at Kaiser Aluminum's Dolton extrusion plant.

The introductory column I wrote for One, *Kaiser's in-house publication.*

Triemstra on Weather

Editor's Note: Roger Triemstra is chief engineer at Kaiser Aluminum's Dolton, Illinois, extrusions plant. He is also a graduate meteorologist and weekend weatherman on Chicago's WGN-TV (see accompanying story). His column, Triemstra on Weather, will appear regularly in One.

The one universal subject that we all discuss at one time or another is the weather. Today we have a national habit of watching the late news on TV prior to retiring, and because of this the local TV weatherman has become as well known as anyone in town. Each of us is interested in his forecast — if not his humor. Additionally, weather, with its peculiarities, has been of major concern to each of us because of its tremendous influence on our lives and its economic impact on the welfare of our society.

We Kaiser Aluminum employees are located from one end of the country to the other, and we can all relate the effects that weather has had on us personally and the tremendous influence that adverse weather conditions have had on our individual plants and offices. The Pacific Northwest and California have experienced extensive drought conditions the last couple of years, the Midwest and Eastern regions experienced the most severe winter in recorded weather history, and those of us in the Gulf Coast regions know the impact that hurricanes have on our operations. The inhabitants of "tornado alley" — an area that extends through Oklahoma, Missouri, southern Illinois, Indiana, and Ohio — are reminded each spring of the potential destruction of nature's most violent storm. And, we in Chicago will never forget the great snowstorm of 1967.

Currently, we see strong evidence that the winter of 1978 will be close to "normal," in that the storms are moving inland along the Pacific Coastal regions and the "storm tracks" in the West and Midwest are bringing more snowfall without the long and severe cold arctic outbreaks. This is good news because it indicates relief for the drought-stricken West and Northwest and less severe temperatures for the Midwest and Eastern regions.

(Editor's note: Since Triemstra wrote this column, the Midwest has been struck by severe blizzards which, says Triemstra, further substantiates earlier evidence.)

I think we can all agree that weather is important to us both in our business and personal lives, and with that premise in mind we introduce this new column to you. Our intent is to inform, educate, and possibly entertain you as we discuss weather features and present information with which you may be only vaguely familiar. We'll discuss weather instruments and their use in forecasting, weather folklore and its relationship to scientific principles, and unusual weather phenomena and their causes, and hopefully some of you will become amateur meteorologists by further study and observation. We're open for suggestions and criticisms with the intent of better informing you — weatherwise.

It's not just the ham in him that inspired Triemstra to work in TV. He has a deep interest in the weather and thinks that's probably true of most people. He's also irritated by the many erroneous reports and forecasts that are taken for gospel by millions of people. "Last winter," he shrugs, "there were guys saying we're heading for another ice age. Talk like that gets people nervous unnecessarily," he says.

"Well, Marty," he concludes his weather report, "winter is coming." As the cameras switch back to the anchorman, Triemstra casually walks out of the studio, returning a few minutes later eating a candy bar. While out, he checks on the score of the Cal-Stanford football game for his West Coast guests, gives the unhappy news to one of them, then returns to the set for the program's conclusion.

He leaves the studio with the rain splashing against the broad grin on his face.

"Okay, buddy," he says, "I was right, wasn't I?"

Just before going on the air, Roger Triemstra reviews last-minute teletype forecasts of the National Weather Service.

I had unique insights because of my knowledge of both meteorology and metallurgy. Kaiser wanted to make sure they weren't making a consumer product that was dangerous. I believe they were trying to be responsible corporate citizens and, because of the many studies into the issue, consumer aerosol products made in the U.S. have not contained ozone-depleting chemicals — also known as chlorofluorocarbons (CFCs) — since the late 1970s, first because companies voluntarily eliminated them, and later because of federal regulations.

I was also moonlighting doing radio and TV weather. If Henry Kaiser's motto was "Find a need and fill it," mine was "Find an opportunity and take it." I did a lot of things, many at the same time, and luckily, the Kaiser bosses didn't mind my weather forecasting. In fact, they liked having a certified meteorologist on staff because I could explain the weather's impact. I was a columnist for Kaiser's in-house publication, *One*, concerning the effects of weather on business.

In the end, though, I was too independent minded for the corporate life. The corporate life has a certain progression you go through, and every time you make an advancement, you give up some freedom. And to me, I always valued my freedom. I was a square peg for a round hole, but my engineering talents were appreciated enough at Kaiser that they put up with my need to explore other areas where my talents could be used.

While I was working full time at Kaiser and part time at WGN-TV, I started doing weather for a Lansing radio station, WLNR, which was a low-power FM station. WLNR stood for "West Lansing Near Railroad." Before I went to Kaiser in the morning, I would drive over to Lansing and give the weather forecast. They thought I was a big deal because I was on Channel 9. I got a few bucks, but I did it more as a favor to my cousin Joe Van Schouwen, who was one of the guys who ran the station.

Joe sold the station in 1991 to Johnson Publishing Company, which changed the call letters to WJPC and changed the format to Urban Adult Contemporary.

A trade newspaper ad placed by Kaiser when I was Manager of Aerosol Customer Services.

Side Hustles

My Triemstra ancestors can be traced back to an area of the northern coast of the Netherlands called Friesland. Descendants are blessed with a strong work ethic, unbreakable determination, and the intelligence to match. Perhaps the best illustration of that was the Frieslanders' repeated efforts to conquer the North Sea. They drained coastal wetlands and made them usable for agriculture and other development by building polders, large embankments to keep out the sea and allow the marshes, which were below sea level, to dry out. Storm after storm would knock down the polders and flood the land and time after time, the Frieslanders would rebuild. They eventually prevailed, as over half of the Netherlands today is on land formerly under water.

I inherited the high energy, risk taking and innate entrepreneurial skills. All of which is to explain why I always had more than one job, or was involved in a variety of entrepreneurial efforts. Two examples are Lynwood Sports Center and Pipes & Pizza in Lansing.

Mick Vanderbilt and I were cousins a couple of times removed — his grandparents and my grandparents were intermarried, and we hung out a lot as we grew up. He called me one day and said, "I'm thinking of building a sports center with a roller rink. You want to build it with me?" I loved roller skating and had an entrepreneurial spirit that went back to selling vegetables out of my wagon, so I was in. That was the first enterprise I did with Mick, and then we bought another roller rink and bowling alley combo in Harvey, Illinois. It needed a lot of upgrading, and we decided it wouldn't be profitable to invest in the improvements, so we sold off the inside contents and made a parking lot for the train station. I guess you could say we paved paradise and put up a parking lot. Mick ran the businesses, and the talent I brought to the businesses was technology, financial awareness, and the ability to obtain finances. Banks knew that if they did business with me, they would get paid back.

The side businesses provided more reasons to travel. Mick and I went to roller skating conventions in the Bahamas and Las Vegas, where Mick wasn't afraid to use the Vanderbilt name to get front-row seats at concerts and other types of treatment a Vanderbilt would be expected to receive. He was a screwball, and we had a lot of fun together over many years, sometimes at my expense. Once, we were water skiing and he was driving the boat. He pulled me over a ski jump, but it was dry, and I had a fin on the back of my ski, so when my skis hit the ramp, I flipped head over heels and back into the water. He got such a laugh out of it he wanted to pull me around again so he could get a picture of my acrobatics.

Lynwood Sport Center opened in 1974 and started out with tennis courts and roller skating, but we ended the tennis part and focused only on roller skating. We sold it in December 1999 to our skating pro, and it's still going strong.

In 1983, I purchased the old Lans Theatre located in Lansing, Illinois, with three of my cousins by marriage: Andrew Vogel, Archie Boomsma and Chuck Zeilstra. It was the same theater Gerrie and I went

Janet Davies and John Drury were among my colleagues who appeared for charity fundraisers at Pipes & Pizza.

to on many dates. We converted the building into Pipes & Pizza and, as the name implies, we served pizza while a professional organist provided the entertainment on a big, old pipe organ. We had a screen drop down and we played silent movies while the organist accompanied the action, had sing-a-longs and took audience requests. The organ was built by the Barton Organ Company in Oshkosh, Wisconsin, and was first installed in 1927 at the Oriental Theatre in Milwaukee. The organ had several homes including a roller rink in Moline, a Minneapolis pizza parlor and a private residence. Pipes & Pizza became a Beggar's Pizza in the early '90s.

The pizza and roller skating businesses were more impressive to my kids and grandkids than my broadcasting career. What's better than your old man owning a pizza place and a roller rink? The kids were there all the time, even working there at times. Our family and friends spent many holidays there, as we opened it up on Thanksgiving and Christmas evenings for private skates.

My love of roller skating began as a child, and when I was the youth leader for our church, I took our group to the skating rink. Here, I was joking around with the girls as they waited to skate.

Mick Vanderbilt and I on one of our many boating excursions.

In 1986, Bozo the Clown and Cooky visited Pipes & Pizza.
INSET: *Roger the Clown.*
BELOW: *Bozo (Bob Bell) and Cooky (Roy Brown) with Gerrie and me.*

Teaching

Teaching was another avocation. I taught economics at IIT and, in a way, my weather forecasting was a form of teaching — but the most meaningful teaching I did involved religion. At church, I taught youth Bible classes and led Bible discussions for adults and, for many years, taught Bible classes behind bars at the Cook County Jail. That jail is a rough, tough place, and while a lot of the men had religious backgrounds, they had fallen away. My goal was for them to understand Jesus Christ, realize they would be forgiven and have a chance to change their lives.

While my classes were based on the Bible, I incorporated a lot of what I read in C.S. Lewis's *Mere Christianity*. I was in my 40s when Vern Boerman, a Bible teacher at Illiana Christian School, introduced me to Lewis's work. Lewis had a way of approaching the Bible intellectually, which helped me with things that are a little hard to swallow, or don't seem to apply to our lives today. He laid things out in a way that made it easier to understand, and that's what I passed along to the inmates.

We had a traditional classroom in the jail, and I prepared homework assignments. That allowed me to make sure that they were reading it, and it let them know someone actually cared and their work mattered. They received grades and at the end of these classes, we had graduation exercises. I wanted the men to understand that even though they had taken a wrong path and done some things that were wrong, they could lead a better life by allowing the Bible to have a positive influence.

Chicagoland Prison Outreach has been sharing the love of Christ with prisoners and families of prisoners since 1994. Its mission is to tangibly communicate the Gospel to Cook County and state prison inmates and their loved ones in a way that gives them real hope and encouragement. To accomplish this goal, in-prison ministries are offered, along with a post-prison ministry and, through partnerships with local churches, several outreach programs.

Travels

I have always gravitated to water — lakes, oceans, streams, pretty much any body of water, so it's no accident so many of my travels involved water. The Great Lakes were frequent targets of my travels: Lake Huron on a trip to Canada, fishing on Lake Erie with my son Dean, Lake Superior for a ski trip, Lake Ontario and the Niagara Falls, and of course, numerous vacations on Lake Michigan. Foreign travels involved oceans, seas and rivers in one way or another.

Our family lake trips are among the most memorable. They started at Silver Lake, near the town of Mears and the Silver Lake Sand Dunes, located along Lake Michigan's sweeping shoreline between Muskegon and Ludington. I started going there as a kid with my sisters and their husbands, and continued spending time there after Gerrie and I married and had kids. The sand dunes along the lake are massive and were turned into a state park in the 1970s. Decades earlier, a newspaper publisher named Swift Lathers built a cluster of cabins he called Dune Forest Village as a retreat. The abandoned shacks, which our family called "The Lost Village," were fun to explore, and getting there under the hot summer sun required running from shade spots to grassy areas of the dunes, to keep from burning your feet, or in my case, my head. The village wasn't much more than shacks and were no match for the shifting sands of the dunes. It was finally removed to make way for a state park.

Swift Lathers also published *The Mears Newz*, known as the smallest newspaper in the world with just four pages measuring in at 5 ¼ by 7 ¼ inches. He decided to start his own paper because he didn't like the constant editing of his work by others and now, he could share his candid comments unedited. We visited his home on occasion and found rooms packed with newspapers, printing presses and quite a character in Mr. Lathers. He featured an article about me in one of the papers, a small blurb in an equally small newspaper.

The "Lost Village" in its final years. Look closely and you can see some Triemstras.

Patti, Cheri and Carl heading for a day in the waters of Silver Lake.

When our children came along, the cabins we'd stay in were very basic, usually just one big room, and we'd hang blankets to create "rooms." No indoor plumbing. We'd spend a week or so there and had great fun with other families we knew who would rent adjacent cabins. Gerrie and the other moms would prepare a week's worth of food at home to take with us. Picnic tables lined up end-to-end served as a smorgasbord for a large, hungry group.

All my children have fond memories of Silver Lake: hiking and sand surfing the dunes, the search for the "Lost Village," swimming in both Silver Lake and Lake Michigan, meeting up with family and friends for our weeklong adventures and the end-of-the week Mac Wood's Dune Rides. When Dean came along, he encouraged more adventurous excursions, which resulted in dune buggies vaulting over a steep cliff and leaving the dads limping and aching for the remainder of the vacation.

Silver Lake was a three-and-a-half-hour drive from our home. The kids were still pretty young then, and as they got older and busier, we wanted to find a place closer to home. Eventually, we bought a cottage on Indian Lake, located just west of Dowagiac, Michigan, one of the Sister Lakes, which was much closer to our home, only about an hour, or so. In fact, I could commute to work from there.

Gerrie and I always made vacations a priority for our family. We spent many weekends snow skiing, water skiing and always planned a weeklong excursion in the summer. One especially memorable trip was to the Lost Valley Dude Ranch located in Sedalia, Colorado, a working guest ranch. There were ranch activities for all ages and our children went off on their own adventures: fly fishing, trapshooting, rodeos, horseback riding, swimming, nightly entertainment, and cookouts.

We visited Tucson, Arizona, frequently since Gerrie's brother and wife lived there, visiting Old Tucson, flea markets, Kitt Peak National Observatory, Saguaro National Park, Sonora Desert among some of the places. And being drawn to water, we did a lot of fishing for salmon on Lake Michigan.

Gerrie heading to the lake from our cabin at Silver Lake.

Our yearly trek to the Lost Village required a shower cap for me, which proved to be more reflective than protective.

Chopping driftwood for firewood at Silver Lake.

We had some great times and close calls on these dune buggies.

Gerrie and Patti walking through one of the channels at Silver Lake.

My sister Ruth with Cheri and Gerrie hiking the sand dunes.

Patti, Carl, Cheri, and cousin Darcy posing on one of many sand dune hikes.

One of the perks of being on radio and television was the travel. The stations discovered they could make money by working with a tour company and setting up listener trips. And to make it attractive for the listeners and viewers to spend their money, various personalities from the stations would lead the tours. For them, the trips were free, but I took it a step further: If you wanted me, you had to pay for Gerrie, too. And they did, time and time again.

A lot of travel was separate from WGN, trips we planned and paid for ourselves, often including family and friends. We saw the world from top to bottom, Gerrie and I always side by side.

On a trip to Antarctica, Gerrie and I were being transported from our ship to shore on a rubber raft.

Ashore, we were greeted by thousands of penguins.

Wherever we traveled I called in weather reports to WGN Radio.
ABOVE: *I'm on a ship-to-shore line from our ship in Antarctica.*
BELOW: *Donning a WGN Radio cap near the bottom of the world.*

Iceberg ahead! Luckily, our captain and crew were paying closer attention than the Titanic's.

Floating down the Amazon River.

ABOVE: *I shared my love of the Chicago White Sox when we visited our ancestral homeland of the Netherlands.*
BELOW: *An Illinois rose among the Holland tulips in 2001.*

ABOVE: *Ready to ride the Alaskan rapids with Don and Jean Spiekhout.*
BELOW: *Gerrie, center, and Marilyn Boomsma with Hugh Graham, owner of Lost Valley Dude Ranch.*

On our 50th wedding anniversary in 2003, Gerrie and I took the whole family — all the kids and grandkids, at least 20 of us — on a cruise up the St. Lawrence Seaway. We were fortunate that we were able to take them on a lot of trips and expand their view of the world.

Gerrie and I were also blessed to have many wonderful dear friends over the years. Many of them we knew since we were kids, and others we met along the way. Many of them joined us on our travels.

Our trip to Alaska with Don and Jean Spiekhout included a long, overnight train ride to Fairbanks, thus the need for a "night shirt." In Fairbanks, we visited the base where Don was stationed.

Trying to catch the big one on one of the Great Lakes.

When Gerrie and I visited Jamaica with our daughter and her husband, we took an excursion on a raft.

Visiting Pima Air and Space Museum in Tucson, Arizona and an example of the bombers I forecast weather for from Lockbourne AFB as they circled the North Pole in the early '50s.

Dean and I on one of our family vacations.

Carl and I at the Grand Canyon.

Patti, Carl and Cheri.

ABOVE LEFT TO RIGHT: *Marv and Carolyn Spender in Hawaii with Gerrie and me.*
LEFT TO RIGHT: *Archie Boomsma, Hans Verbeek, Don Spiekhout and me.*

ABOVE: *Marv Spender and I in Cancun.*

BELOW: *One of the many times Tom Beishuizen and I waited as our wives shopped.*

Carl Boender and I at a Chicago White Sox game.
BELOW LEFT TO RIGHT: *Some of the "Skiing Dutchmen." Dick and Pet Kuiper, Gerrie, and Marv and Carolyn Spender.*

We had a group of 10 or 12 couples who went on ski trips together. We called ourselves the "Skiing Dutchmen." We'd ski all day, and then at night we'd put on shows, such as the one pictured below. We played games and just had a great time. Gerrie wasn't as into the skiing as I was, but she liked the social aspect, and really liked the outfits, such as the green one she's wearing in the photo taken at one of the many resorts we visited.

Gerrie and I enjoyed many sunsets. This photo of us at Silver Lake was one of her favorites.

The Cottage

One of our best purchases was the lake property in southwest Michigan. I was doing better then, and we wanted to find a place that we could buy and was closer to home and Chicago. The kids were getting older and were having their own children, so we wanted a place where we could all spend vacation time together. We had a chance to buy a property on Indian Lake, a large, inland lake just off the southeast tip of Lake Michigan, just east of Stephensville, Michigan.

We referred to it as "The Cottage," but there were actually two cabins on the property. We used the main cabin for adults and the other for the kids, grandkids, and other visitors. Gerrie and I enjoyed entertaining and that was a great spot for it. The property was right on the water and had a dock. We were fortunate to have dozens of our family, friends and WGN colleagues join us over the years.

The cottage on Indian Lake.

Our cottage home — the front one for the adults and the back one for the kids and grandkids.

I winterized the cottages so we could enjoy them year round.

In 1991, we hosted a big Fourth of July party with colleagues from WGN and other friends who celebrated with us.

Sharon and Lyle Dean on the swings with John Tondelli. Lyle was a WGN newsman and John was record turner and music director for the station.
BELOW: *Spike and I lean in for a shot.*

Part of the Morning Show group: Anne Maxfield, Spike, me and Tracy Hueverman.

We had many fun times hosting friends at our Indian Lake cottage. Gerrie and me, Hans and Jo Verbeek, Marilyn and Archie Boomsma.

ABOVE: *Hans Verbeek and me.*
BELOW: *Frank Groen, me, Harold DeBoer, Don Spiekhout, Archie Boomsma and Hans Verbeek.*

One may surmise by the number of times I was photographed napping that it was a common occurrence. Perhaps.

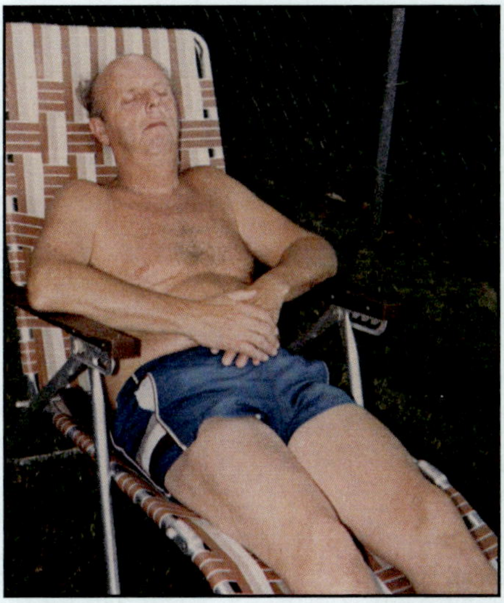

Above: *Kaitlyn Powell fishing off the dock at Indian Lake.*
Below: *Taking some of the grandkids for a spin.*

Jakob Triemstra and I comb the beach at Lake Michigan.

Apple picking was a fun activity each fall with the grandkids. AT RIGHT: *Rachel Triemstra and I pick apples from a tree tagged with Bob Collins' name on it.* BELOW: *Jakob Triemstra and I fill up our bag.*

Legacy

Family has always been the top priority and my hope is that Gerrie and I provided the best opportunities for our children to succeed in whatever ways they define success. But, parenting is a bit like farming and gardening: You do your best to provide the best growing conditions and nutrients, both physical and spiritual. You nurture the seedlings and hope nature will be generous. Gerrie and I were blessed with four children, 13 grandchildren and 15 great-grandchildren.

Parenting is also analogous to forecasting the weather. As a meteorologist, I knew what the atmospheric conditions and data told me the approaching weather *should* be, but now and then Ma Nature threw a curveball and let me know I wasn't in charge. In that regard, the Triemstra family is no different than any other family. We had our share of sunny days with joys and blessings, and we also had storms with tragedies and sorrows.

In a perfect world, a parent would not have to bury a child, nor a grandparent a grandchild. That's not the natural order of how life is supposed to go. Sometimes that order is broken. We buried three of our grandchildren.

Our first-born grandson, Adam Richard Powell, passed away at the young age of 7 1/2 months. At first, doctors thought it could have been because of SIDS because there were no signs of anything wrong. But testing showed he had a rare genetic disorder that affects infants and children called endocardial fibroelastosis (EFE). The heart muscle thickens when the fibers and tissues of the heart expand, and it is too much for the heart wall to contain.

My daughter Patti and son-in-law Rick were living in Tucson, Arizona, at the time, and Gerrie's brother and wife also lived there, which proved to be such a blessing that they could be there for support. Memorial services were held in Tucson for Adam, and his body would

Gerrie and I with our first grandchild, Adam.

be flown back to Illinois for burial and a service would be held for family there. Rick would eventually be transferred back to the Chicago area, so this was their choice for burial. I flew back to Chicago and was met at the airport by the funeral director, who was also a close friend and neighbor. Patti and Rick flew separately, and since my daughter was pregnant at the time with Katy, they went to visit the burial site after the memorial was over. We drove to the burial site, and I was overwhelmed with kindness

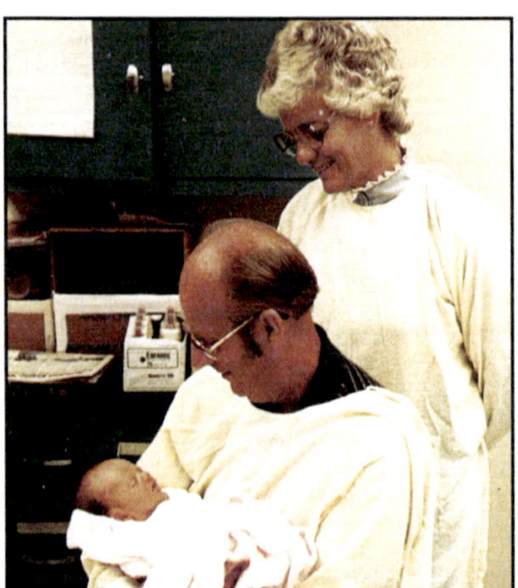

Gerrie and I with little Katy.

as friends and members of our church showed up to support me during this difficult time, burying our first-born grandson.

When Katy was born, she was diagnosed with the same disorder as Adam. Katy was monitored very closely, but passed when she was only four months old. Again, we were devastated and did our best to support Patti and Rick.

Other grandchildren were being born and Patti and Rick adopted two baby boys, Joshua and Aaron. We had many family get-togethers and vacations where all of our grandchildren were present — our favorite memories.

Patti became pregnant with Bethany and the doctors reassured her the odds were in her favor that this child would not carry the same genetic disorder her other children carried, but that was not to be true. Bethany lived to be 18 months, passing away after a heart transplant.

Patti and Rick were warriors and their deep faith carried them through this ordeal that seemed to never end. They have three children, adopting Kaitlyn, a little girl from Korea, and now also have five grandchildren. I am so proud of them and how they have lived their life to the fullest, despite the incredible losses they suffered through.

Bethany Powell

Being on television and radio provides an extension of your family and another layer of caring. People who see and listen to you become aware of your joys and sorrows and respond in kind. I received many kind notes and condolences from the audience and they were greatly appreciated.

Our 13 grandchildren blessed us with 15 great-grandchildren. We have so many wonderful memories of family gatherings, weddings, graduations, band concerts and many grandparents' days.

After I retired, I was able to spend a lot of time with the local grandkids. I had a Buick Electra station wagon, and I would pick these kids up and take them to three or four different parks to play. One park had a World War II tank and they'd climb all over it. Then we'd pile in the car and go get a sack of sliders and ice cream. I don't know if their parents knew what I was doing with them, but the kids sure loved it and so did I. And remember, by that time, I certainly wasn't a kid anymore, I must have been 65, but that was an important part of their life and my life that they still remember.

Most of the family still lives in Illinois and Indiana with others scattered in North Carolina, Michigan and Florida.

Rachel and Meghan at the cottage.

Aaron Powell and Grandpa Roger.

We had a lot of birthday parties. Shown are Meghan, Aaron, Joshua, and Rachel.

In Grandpa's arms. LEFT: *Meghan and Rachel* RIGHT: *Aaron and Joshua*

Two photos of Joshua Powell and me.
ABOVE: *Happy Joshua.* BELOW: *Not-so-happy Joshua.*

Dean and I during his baseball team's trip to the WGN-TV studio.

Aaron, Meghan, Josh, Rachel. I went from peddling vegetables and lemonade around South Holland in my wagon as a boy to pulling grandkids around.

Son Carl and I at my grandson Justin Triemstra's graduation.

Granddaughter Rachel Triemstra on her wedding day to Brian Bardolph.

Griffin's graduation from the Coast Guard Academy.

Zachary's graduation.

ABOVE: *Attending a Halloween party with Lilly and Jakob.*
BELOW: *The grandkids are ready for treats.*

LEFT TO RIGHT: *Jessa and me, Grace, Gerrie with Stella, and Izzy.*
BELOW: *Adam Powell and Bethany Powell.*

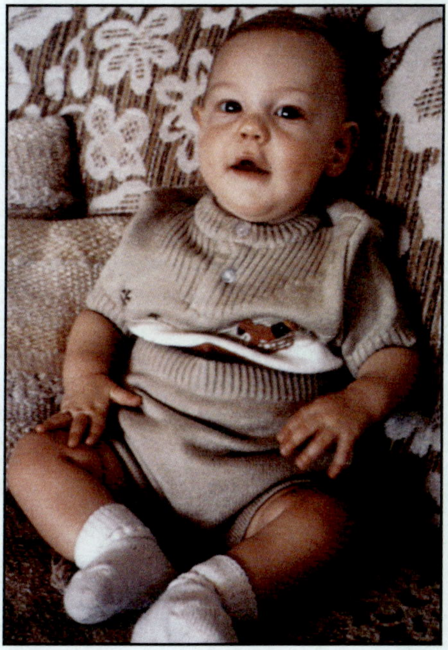

Katy Powell

Gerrie is holding Kaitlyn, and standing in front are Joshua and Aaron Powell.

Grandparents Day at Izzy's school.

Lilly with Grandpa.

At our South Holland home: Patti, Cheri, Gerrie, Carl, me and Dean.

Christmas 1961 Gerrie, Cheri, Carl and Patti.

Questions From the Family

Patti and Rick Powell, daughter and son-in-law
What extracurricular activities were you involved with in high school?

I was involved in many high school extracurricular activities, but they were different than the typical ones that are in high schools today. I was a hall monitor, a bus monitor, and I became the cafeteria cashier, which was instrumental in teaching me my math skills. I excelled in school and I was a member of the honors club. One outside organization I belonged to was the youth YMCA (Young Men's Christian Association). This group was organized so Christian principles would be encouraged for the youth of public schools.

Rick and Patti Powell with grandchildren Walter, Henry, Christian, Sydney and Nadine.

Josh Powell, grandson

Who are the first five people you want to meet in heaven besides your wife?

I have lived a long life and have experienced many losses. Many of my lifelong friends are no longer on this earth; my sisters and their husbands and my in-laws and their husbands have passed on, as well. I have also experienced the devastating loss of three of my dear grandchildren. With each person's passing, I am left with beautiful memories of the life they lived and the life I shared with them. Upon my arrival in heaven, I am looking forward to seeing my parents again. I had wonderful memories of my childhood and my parents were always a great support to me. Gerrie's parents were like my own parents and we experienced a close bond, and I am also looking forward to seeing them in heaven. C.S. Lewis was an inspirational person in my life and his writings changed my core belief system. I would love to see him in heaven and discuss his writings.

Josh and Sarah Powell with children Walter and Nadine.

Sarah Powell, granddaughter-in-law
What singular book from the Bible has the Lord revealed the most to you?

Without a doubt, the Book of James. James was Jesus's brother, and his book was one of the smallest in the Bible. I have always enjoyed the Book of James because it gives instructions and guidance on how Christians should live their life. It never seemed to me like "ancient writings," more like it could have been written last week, very contemporary. Also, the Book of James is one of the books that is consistent among the various versions of the Bible. And it is not flowery prose, but direct and to the point, which I enjoy.

Walter Powell, great-grandson
What is the coolest place you've traveled to, and why?

When Gerrie and I traveled to Antarctica and the Arctic/Alaska, we went for scientific purposes and weather exploration, and it was truly a great trip to go on. We gathered a group of people together who were listeners of WGN and planned this trip. While in Antarctica, we saw enormous glaciers, rode in rubber boats to shore to see the penguins and, I still did my Chicago weather forecasts back to WGN. We also visited a scientific station that evaluated the levels of the ozone layer and tracked its depletion. In the Arctic/Alaska, we visited small towns in the area, went rafting down a river and went on a lot of explorations.

Walter Powell

Nadine Powell, great-granddaughter
What is one of your favorite memories with a friend when you were a kid?

One of my favorite memories is playing softball. I was on a church league from Bethany Church with my sister Emily's husband, Mike Van Zuidam. I also enjoyed winter sports quite a bit. I did a lot of sledding and once the ponds in the area froze over, you could find me ice skating or catching a game of hockey with my friends.

Nadine Powell

Aaron and Leah Powell holding Henry and Sydney.

Aaron and Leah Powell, grandson and granddaughter-in-law

What did you find to be the most technical advance in meteorology during your career?

Radar was the most technical advance that I saw in my weather career. Prior to having radar, there were no warnings for hurricanes, tornados or any other serious weather systems, so no alerts were sent out to people to shelter or evacuate prior to these storms. Also, we were not aware of the jet streams, and once they were discovered, we were able to accurately forecast for airplane pilots and smoothly navigate their flight patterns. In WWII, the planes would take off from ocean islands and were sent to bomb Japan. They were flying east to west at 150 miles per hour, and the jet stream is from the west to the east, causing the bombs to miss their targets and scatter before they reached the ground. The jet stream headwinds required the bombers to use far more fuel than expected and at times they ran out of fuel on the return flights.

Gerrie and I danced with Aaron and Leah at their wedding.

One of the Buick Electra wagons.

Henry and Sydney Powell, great-grandchildren
What was your favorite vehicle owned?

Without a doubt, my Buick Electra Station wagon. In fact, I owned two of them. And I loved these cars, not for their design, or speed, or reliability — I loved them because I could fit all my grandchildren in them, and at the time I had these cars, I had eight grandchildren. We would often all pile into the car, and I would drive them to the "tank park" and afterwards to get some sliders and ice cream. Those days still hold some of my most precious memories.

Sydney Powell

Henry Powell

Christian and Kaitlyn Powell

Faith and Carl Triemstra with granddaughter Clara Bardolph.

Christian Powell, great-grandson
If you could own one more car, what would it be and why?

To me, automobiles are primarily a means of transportation — point A to point B. I chose my cars based on practicality, how many people could fit in, safety, and towing capacity because I owned boats and jet skis that I pulled to numerous lakes and eventually our cottage. As a child, I was drawn to convertible cars, but my practicality never allowed me to purchase one.

Kaitlyn Powell, granddaughter
What is one of the biggest lessons you took from serving in the Korean War?

That war causes death, destruction, and many widows and orphans among a long list of other undesirables. I believe more in negotiation, mediation, and arbitration if possible. That is the biggest lesson I took from serving in the Korean War and have witnessed in numerous wars and conflicts since then. Obviously, I understand the need at times to take a strong stance when our country is attacked, but if war and all the atrocities that come with it can be avoided, I support other options.

Carl Triemstra, son
What advice would you like to pass along to your family's youngest generation?

I would think the best advice I could give to my grandchildren and great-grandchildren was consistently present throughout my life. I have always had Christian faith and raised my family in this same faith. It becomes a personal way of life, so the first piece of advice would be to have Jesus in your heart and show that in the life you choose. In my work life and professional career, I generally kept this at the top of my mind when I made decisions. Additional advice is to be willing to take a chance in life and step out of your comfort zone. I lived this from childhood on and it served me well.

Faith Triemstra, daughter-in-law

How did the teaching position at IIT come about? How many years teaching? Did you teach micro or macroeconomics? Why that subject?

I was always interested in teaching and since I was an alumnus of the Illinois Institute of Technology, I reached out to see if there were any open teaching positions. It was a great opportunity for additional income doing something I enjoyed. I taught both macro and microeconomics and Paul Samuelson, the author of the book I taught from, and who taught at MIT, was very engineering orientated, which suited me. I would tell my students that if they saw me on television, it was the same guy teaching their class.

Rachel, Brian, Calvin, Clara and Lucas Bardolph

Brian and Rachel Bardolph, granddaughter and grandson-in-law
What's one thing you're proud of that and you've never told anyone about?

When I was growing up and through some of my adult life, I have shown a scratchy surface, a rough nature and some questionable humor. It was my go-to behavior, and it was part of the radio schtick on WGN. As I have grown older, experienced more life and settled into retirement, I have developed a kinder and a softer heart. I still have a "way" about me, but I have more rounded edges now. I am proud that I became aware of this and have worked on my character.

Clara and twins Calvin and Lucas, my great-grandchildren.

Clara and Calvin and Lucas Bardolph, great-grandchildren
Who was your best friend as a child, and tell us a story about him/her?

When I was a child, I never had a specific best friend, but a lot of friends in general. We hung out in groups and did group activities like roller skating, baseball games or going to parades and festivals.

Emma, Rachel, Justin and Peter Triemstra

Peter and Emma

When I became older, I developed stronger, closer friendships and my strongest friendships were with Don Spiekhout, Archie Boomsma, Smitty (Henry Smit) and Chuck Jacobsma. Gerrie and I went on numerous vacations with couples like Tom and Ceil Beishuizen, Hans and Jo Verbeek, Mick and Jane Vanderbilt and Marv and Carolyn Spender and these relationships I always enjoyed. I recently have developed strong friendships with others like Carl Boender and Jack Elzinga and some of my card buddies at Hartsfield Village, where I live.

Justin and Rachel Triemstra, grandson and granddaughter-in-law
What was your hardest job and why?

My hardest job was working the onion sets as a child. It was tough work, long hours, very hot and not very rewarding. I knew that this was not the life I wanted as an adult, so the Air Force, education and taking opportunities when they were presented to me were my ways to choose a life path that eliminated manual labor. As an adult though, I worked in my yard and at the cottage with the same energy I did in the fields. I always took pride in how my lawn and flowers looked, and this was directly related to my farm work as a child.

Peter and Emma, great-grandchildren

Besides painting your red wagon black, what else did you do with it?

There were not a lot of outdoor toys on my dad's farm, so when I received my wagon as a gift, I was very excited. I would pull neighbor kids around in it or they would push me around in it. But when I was a bit older and had the capacity to realize I could make a few cents for myself, I would deliver vegetables or groceries to the neighbor ladies or bring lemonade to the workers down the road from my house. But I always wished I could have left it black and not scrub off the paint to return it to the red color.

Four generations: Cheri, Gerrie holding Isabelle, Meghan.

Cheri Triemstra, daughter

I have had consistent passions throughout my life, but my hobbies have changed as my interests evolve. What were your consistent passions and hobbies throughout your life?

Reading, teaching, roller skating and ice skating. Since I was one of the smallest kids in my class growing up, I never participated in the team sports such as football or basketball. I preferred individual sports which didn't really require size or muscle but more balance and coordination, which I had. So, I was drawn to ice skating and roller skating. We would ice skate on frozen ponds growing up and when I was in high school, we would all gather at the local roller skating rink located in Lansing, Illinois. I also had a love for reading, which to this day, is something I really enjoy. I was also always drawn to teaching — teaching Sunday School, adult Bible classes, and economics at IIT as an adult. On occasion, I was asked to speak in schools or to other organizations on the topic of weather, and I always said yes to these opportunities since I enjoyed it so much.

Izzy Kus and Meghan Terpstra

Izzy Kus

Meghan Terpstra, granddaughter
If you could have lived in a different era, what era would it be and why?

Without a doubt, I would choose the Pre-Depression, the '20s and the '30s. It might seem odd to choose an era that is less advanced and, by appearance, a harder life. But, in my opinion, it was a more carefree and fun time, a simpler life. There was also less technology and you depended on the human mind and not computers to solve problems. This might seem a bit archaic, but I enjoyed using and depending on my own brain and not the computer.

Izzy Kus, great-granddaughter
What is your favorite sport to play and to watch?

My favorite sport to play was tennis. In South Holland, we had a tennis court behind our house in the park, and I spent hours playing tennis with my children, who later joined the high school tennis teams, and I enjoyed a game with Gerrie a time or two. I would also challenge some of my neighbors to a game and would always love to see if I could beat some of my sons' friends at a game. My favorite game to watch is golf. While I never played much golf growing up or as an adult, it is a very interesting game and enjoyable to watch on television.

Zachary Terpstra, grandson
What was your favorite thing about Grandma?

I probably could write a separate book just to answer this question and I could never just choose one thing that was my favorite thing about her. We enjoyed a wonderful and adventurous life and she loved me with no restrictions. She loved her children and provided an amazing homelife for them, and she adored her grandchildren and great-grandchildren. The joy she had when being with them was palpable. She also had a lovely disposition and was the sweetest person I knew. The tributes received at her wake reflected her character and how gracious and loving she was.

With Zachary at one of my favorite places: a White Sox game.

Grace and Jessa Terpstra

Jessa Terpstra, great-granddaughter
What is your favorite cloud and why?

The cumulonimbus cloud. It is the most majestic of clouds and it gives us the most moisture for the earth. It is associated with heavy rain, torrential downpours, hailstorms, lightening and even tornadoes. At times, these clouds are referred to as thunderheads and are a dense, towering vertical cloud, forming from water vapor carried by powerful upward air currents. Take a look in the sky some time and see if you can recognize them.

Grace Terpstra, great-granddaughter
If you could be an animal, what would it be and why?

A horse. I always loved ponies when I was a child, and on the farms I worked on there were always horses, either for farm work or for pleasure riding. They are very enjoyable animals; every horse has its own personality, and I was never afraid of them. I loved being around them and later in life, I took my family to a dude ranch in Colorado for a week-long immersion into horse riding and dude ranch life.

Circa 1947 in Colorado.

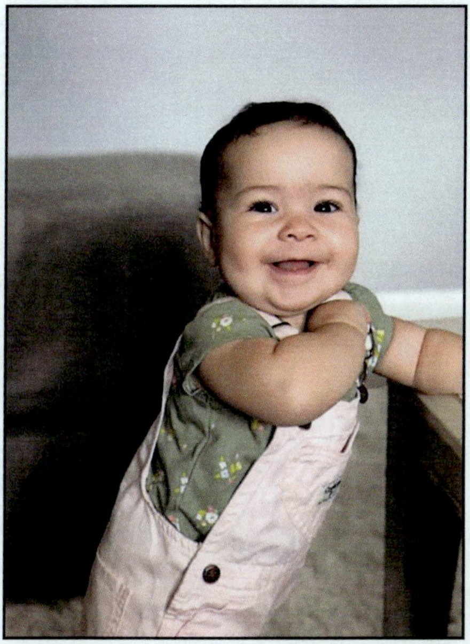

Above: *Willa and Stella Terpstra.*
Below: *With parents Tiffany and Griffin Terpstra.*

Griffin Terpstra, grandson
Why is a duck?

A standing tradition with my grandkids were nonsensical jokes. I would tell them some joke that made no sense and they would come up with some funny answers, but mostly they were confused and unsure of their response. But we always had a good laugh over the jokes. The answer to "Why is a duck?" Because one of his feet are both alike. See? It makes no sense.

Tiffany Terpstra, granddaughter-in-law
Who had the biggest influence on your life and why?

The author, C.S. Lewis. He is most known for his book about the children's fantasy *The Lion, the Witch, and the Wardrobe*, later writing six additional stories becoming the series *The Chronicles of Narnia*. But the book that influenced me was *Mere Christianity.* I was raised as a conservative Christian by my parents, but C.S. Lewis's writings made me understand who Jesus Christ was and I became a Christian because of the Lewis book and his explanation of Christianity.

Stella and Willa Terpstra, great-grandchildren
What is your favorite kind of ice cream?

I am not a big ice cream or dessert person, but my favorite ice cream treat is vanilla with chocolate sauce, topped with whipped cream and a cherry. But my favorite dessert is lemon meringue pie — and the best kind is made with real lemon gelatin and real egg whites!

Dean with Gerrie and me.

Jakob Triemstra

Lilly Triemstra

Dean Triemstra, son
What business venture are you most proud of?

Walking the Bible. That was a project with author Bruce Feiler, who walked where Jesus walked and wrote a book about it. Bruce wanted to create a television series and put it on PBS and make it a best-selling book. It was exciting for me. I enjoyed the book, loved the concept and the challenge of finding investors and organizing the group that took it to PBS. We attracted 20 investors and raised $3 million.

Jakob Triemstra, grandson
What is the biggest difference between the world you grew up in and the world today?

The biggest difference between the world I grew up in and the world today is technology and the speed at which technology advances. I have a computer, a Facebook portal and even a smart TV and do enjoy the advances that technology provides me through these devices — but I can barely operate them, nor correct an issue if they don't work properly. I rely on others to solve the problems. I watch my great-grandchildren operate devices expertly and know that this is the future that I would rather not be a part of. I am at a loss when it comes to today's technology.

Lilly Triemstra, granddaughter
What do you feel are the most important things you learned in school?

Enjoyment of reading and mastering mathematics, which have both served me well throughout my life. I am an avid reader of many different genres and love to pick up a book and immerse myself in the story line. I also learned in school to master mathematics and can still calculate most math problems in my head. Old school math and problem solving always was a favorite subject of mine.

A lineup of descendants at Six Flags.

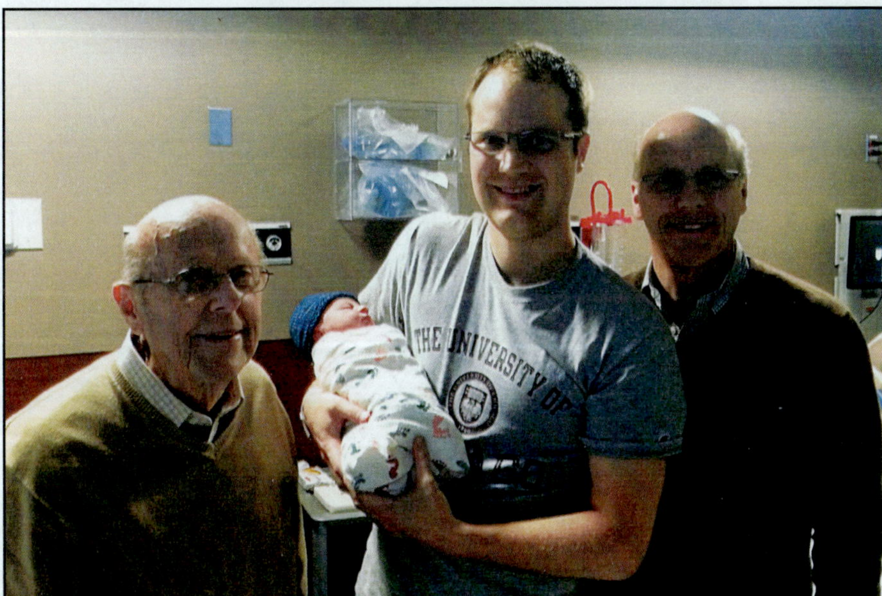

Four generations:
Me, great-grandson Peter, grandson Justin, and son Carl.

I had already retired by the time this photo with Jakob was taken, but had I still been on the job, I'm sure I would have forecast the snow.

ABOVE: *At the cottage with Lilly Triemstra.*
RIGHT: *I was happy to step in as a Bible character with Rachel.*

The Family of
Roger and Gerrie Triemstra

Patti (daughter) and Rick Powell
Son Joshua and wife Sarah Powell (Walter and Nadine)
Son Aaron and wife Leah Powell (Henry and Sydney)
Daughter Kaitlyn Powell (Christian)
Deceased children Adam, Katy, and Bethany

Carl (son) and Faith Triemstra
Daughter Rachel and Brian Bardolph
(Clara, Calvin and Lucas)
Son Justin and Rachel Triemstra (Peter and Emma)

Cheri Triemstra (daughter)
Daughter Meghan Terpstra (Izzy Kus)
Son Zachary Terpstra (Grace and Jessa)
Son Griffin and wife Tiffany Terpstra
(Stella and Willa)

Dean Triemstra (son)
Son Jakob Triemstra and daughter Lilly Triemstra

The Final Chapter

My final chapter is not yet written. As of the writing of this book, I am 91 years old. I am sure of the ending, though. I will greet my Lord and Savior in heaven, reunite with my life partner, my lovely bride, Gerrie, and no longer feel the pains this old body has carried. I trust the next chapter because the Author has planned my life.

> *Blessed is the man who remains steadfast under trial, for when he has stood the test he will receive the crown of life, which God has promised to those who love him.* James 1:12

Acknowledgments

Writing a book at 91 was ambitious on my part. When I set out to tell my story, I knew this was going to be different than anything I'd done before; I knew I was not a writer, and my prose was more technical than storytelling. I would like to acknowledge the extraordinary debt I owe to my co-writers, Diane Montiel and Steve Alexander from Bantry Bay Publishing, for taking a recording of garbled words and scattered thoughts and turning it into a story of my life that I can share with family and friends. For your endless patience and encouragement and being there as I traveled back in my memories to recall long forgotten adventures, I thank you.

I also didn't realize the amount of behind the scenes work this project would take: the weekly interview calls, the search for pictures to add life to my stories, the review of chapters to make sure my words were accurately conveyed and that the final result reflected the vision I had. Overseeing, managing and implementing all of that was my daughter Cheri Triemstra, and I am deeply indebted to her. And to the many family members who supported the effort and contributed to it with their stories questions and photos, I'm very grateful.

I certainly can't forget to acknowledge colleagues Tom Skilling and Spike O'Dell for their support and contributions to this book. Thanks, fellas!

To my future readers, some I have met and others I never will, thank you for picking up a book about an old meteorologist and how life can take twists and turns that change your life. Find your opportunity and take it.

Finally, I would like to thank God for guiding me through all the difficulties, for experiencing your guidance day by day, for the great happiness I have had in my life and for the days I have left to live.